Jane Field-Lewis is an award-winning stylist and art director working in photography, film and TV. She is the author of the My Cool series of lifestyle and interior books. She is also the creator, creative consultant and stylist behind the hit British TV series *Amazing Spaces.* She lives in London.

THE

ANATOMY

OF

SHEDS

THE ANATOMY OF SHEDS

NEW BUILDINGS FROM AN OLD TRADITION

JANE FIELD-LEWIS

GIBBS SMITH
TO ENRICH AND INSPIRE HUMANKIND

First published in the United Kingdom in 2016 by
Pavilion, 1 Gower Street, London WC1E 6HD

Copyright © 2017 Pavilion Books Company Ltd.
Text copyright © 2017 Jane Field-Lewis

Published in the United States of America by
Gibbs Smith
PO Box 667
Layton, Utah 84041

1.800.835.4993 orders
www.gibbs-smith.com

ISBN 978-1-4236-4718-8
Library of Congress Control Number: 2016945732

Printed and bound in China

21 20 19 18 17   5 4 3 2 1

CONTENTS

INTRODUCTION

Over the past few years a very simple phenomenon has given rise to creative ambitions that take the traditional backyard shed or cabin way beyond its origins. Small space design, a growing trend for more simple architectural structures and the emergence of the "shed" aesthetic have converged to provide a unique way for us to express ourselves as individuals. Partly born from the recessionary need to achieve more with less, this trend has taken root with people from all income groups and skill sets. The result is a rich cultural seam of backyard offices and studios, art installations and even serious architectural pieces of work, all with a small footprint.

As a stylist I have spent the best part of my career looking at style in context, whether it's a character in a film script or an image that conveys a mood or atmosphere. Style out of context is only half the story and somewhat empty, but when it's combined with personality it can be magical. By integrating what I do – styling, art directing and writing – into a book format, I have now written over 10 books. This is my second on the subject of "sheds." The first, *my cool shed*, turned into a bestseller and a bit of a trailblazer and struck a chord with many people. It evolved and grew into the international hit Channel 4 TV series *George Clarke's Amazing Spaces* with its unusual and quirky subject matter, an emphasis on visual style and a delicious combination of design and humanity.

Looking back at that extraordinary journey and having encountered so many owners of incredible "sheds" along the way, I realize now that my task is still not finished. Indeed, the story has grown, along with the numbers of shed creators, dwellers, designers, artists and businesses, and it's only partly told. The "shed" phenomenon has expanded and inspired an increasing number of creative folk, and, consequently, there are many more "cool sheds" out there with owners who are willing to tell their tales.

Within the context of this book I invite you to explore some more amazing sheds, both practically and inspirationally. The purpose and passion that went into creating them are there to be seen and read about. Whether it's vernacular, small-scale architecture, creative building by courageous owners looking for another way to express themselves or even change their lives, or simple cabins, garden sheds, studios and trailers, geodesic domes and ice huts, there are examples of them all in the following pages. The cost of these builds, from no budget at all to sizeable sums, is immaterial; the value for their creators cannot be measured in monetary terms. Some are works of art, whereas others are family homes, places of retreat or successful businesses. Some are strikingly architectural in form while others are roughly hewn or highly finished. The canvas is broad and almost anything goes.

My plan was to curate an eclectic selection featuring a diverse range of styles, sources and purposes but all inspirational in their own way. It could be a small detail that fires your imagination, such as the texture of a material, or a big concept that fuels your own plans for shed building. Of course, it's not just physical inspiration that this book offers, it's human stories, too, like the young couple setting up a fledgling business or the artist creating a gallery-worthy piece of work – each lovely build has its own personal and interesting story to tell. And that's where the title concept – the "anatomy" of sheds – becomes

BACKYARD

The dream of owning our very own backyard shed can motivate our creativity and encourage us to find innovative solutions to the problem of creating practical spaces in our homes. The sheds featured here have a variety of uses and function as home offices, workshops, rented accommodation, chill-out spaces and even a cinema. Practical yet inspirational, they each have their own individual aesthetic appeal and delight us with their ingenuity and style.

Caitlin Long's San Francisco home office started out as a typical garden tool shed but is now a stylish space with a strong aesthetic, where she can work or hang out with family and friends. Further up the coast in Seattle is an elegant yet practical reinvention of a potting shed. It blends seamlessly into its surroundings and even has a green roof to camouflage it from above. And inspired by "bacon and tomato sandwiches, fresh salads and dill pickles," a retired engineer used locally sourced reclaimed materials to hand build his own remarkable greenhouse in Nova Scotia for growing organic vegetables.

Across the pond in England, the architect Ben Davidson has created one of the most precise garden sheds ever made. His model-making workshop was designed to fit around the workbench and tools he inherited from his grandfather, a talented carpenter. He likes it so much that it is now the prototype for the sheds he designs for his clients. There's even an "impossible" shed in a London back garden that's used as a cinema, projection space and studio. To comply with local planning legislation, it was cleverly designed to have two stories housed within a one-story exterior. Visually striking and dynamic in its conception, it works on a practical level as well as being full of surprises.

You can turn your back garden into a thriving business, as illustrated by the writer J. Wes Yoder's Nashville vintage trailer. With only basic DIY skills, he did all the restoration work himself and transformed it into a cool "guest room" with a bathhouse and outdoor shower. In no time at all he had bookings for weeks ahead and it earns him rental income. And a serial shed-building artist from Scotland used salvaged scaffolding boards, tin roofing and glass from a dismantled conservatory to build a very special tree house with far-ranging views over the surrounding countryside, and now rents it out to passing cyclists. Who would have thought that the humble backyard shed could be manifested in so many styles and guises?

BACKYARD SHED

Describing herself as the mother of two boys and a creative type who likes making things, a DIYer and blogger about her house and projects, San Francisco resident Caitlin Long keeps herself busy. Her 100 sq ft (9.3 sq m) repurposed and renovated garden shed is used by her family for everything from "late night studying to early morning business calls."

THE STRUCTURE

This typical garden shed, which was built for storing gardening tools and supplies, is tucked into a rear corner of a San Francisco backyard that is 25 ft (7.6 m) wide and 125 ft (38 m) long. It was designed originally to be a functional space for tidying away implements and equipment that were a bit of an eyesore. The structure is relatively new – it was finished in 2008 – and it measures 10 x 10 ft (3 x 3 m). These dimensions are important: any larger and in this city the shed would be classed as a second dwelling requiring a permit. Its rear two corners are made up from the flat concrete retaining wall at the end of the plot, which is built into a hill.

RENOVATION AND TRANSFORMATION

The original shed walls that abutted the structural wall at the back of the garden were concrete, dank and cold, and the shed had become a "spider-infested repository for junk." Caitlin embarked on a renovation project and, over a six-week build schedule, with her husband and elder son helping her, she lined the concrete walls with cedar and installed a small portable wood-burning stove. Immediately, the shed felt warmer and more cozy, so much so that soon afterwards she decided to convert it "into a workspace where my kids could hang out and my husband could take business calls away from the noise of the house." In practical terms this meant purging the shed of all its accumulated junk and relocating most of the garden tools to the garage. Caitlin vacuumed away the spiders' webs and washed all the surfaces with TSP (trisodium phosphate) prior to painting them.

THE PLAN

Caitlin's objective was to turn the shed into a comfortable yet unfussy space. It needed to function and look like a genuine workspace – a home office – as well as being a good place to hang out. Her aesthetic vision was "a gentleman's club vibe without looking too theme-ish or clichéd. I wanted to buy as little as possible while fitting the room out nicely."

Inspired by the style of gentleman's clubs, the vertical cedar paneling and the distressed leather chair add warmth, sophistication and depth to the interior, making it a pleasant place to hang out.

crystal clear. We all appreciate that most great ideas and achievements come from a blend of inspirational sources and experiences, but rather than just describe each constituent part we look in detail at how they interact and relate to one another: the design inspiration, the owner, the build, the practicalities and, above all, that joyous moment when they all happily collide and a great idea comes to life.

Photographically, in an Instagram-fueled world, everyone's eye is becoming more highly attuned to a great image, and in this book I've returned to my familiar milieu of high-end photography to share these delights with you. I've chosen large-scale images that engage and delight, and for some of the sheds featured, I've stepped out of my comfort zone as I believe passionately that people's talents are wider than they often imagine. With this in mind, I persuaded some talented shed creators to pick up a camera and shoot their projects themselves. As a result, it's been an enlightening and richly rewarding experience.

This book is a hybrid, positioned somewhere among and between the genres of interiors, architecture, lifestyle, design guides and storybooks. I leave it to you to take your pick and enjoy the mix. As ever, I am just the conduit and translator – without the contributors and shed creators these pages would be empty. As John Falvey, one of the craftsman shed owners, said about his own work: "People appreciate having their attention guided to what they have not noticed and seeing something constructed carefully and well." It's a quiet opinion, offered gently and generously. Hopefully you can share in their joy, too, and find your own inspiration somewhere within the following pages.

Here goes . . .

SKILLS

It always helps if you love what you do, and never more so than with practical, creative projects. With a background in antique restoration and a degree in furniture design and building from Rhode Island School of Design, Caitlin had not only the technical skills but also the vision and flair to tackle this build.

MATERIALS AND DECORATION

The cedar paneling adds great warmth and depth to the interior of this humble little shed with its concrete slab floor. The easy-to-install cedar cladding is tongue and groove, and behind that - in front of the concrete - is a grid of insulating wood, 2 x 4 in (5 x 10 cm) and with an easy nailing surface. Caitlin wanted to incorporate some softer finishes to make the shed feel less austere and more homely. Throwing some vintage rugs on the floor really warms this space up. As she says, "I find that old Persian rugs are impervious to dirt, so they're great for a space like this. And adding other textures to the room keeps it warm and visually interesting." The wood stove works very effectively in this little space. Who doesn't like a real fire? And decorating with highly personal objects and art makes the room feel authentic.

COLOR PALETTE AND TEXTURES

In its previous existence as a humble garden shed, it was painted a stark white, which looked quite bleak in the daylight and felt sterile and cold. However, Caitlin is a fan of the decorator Abigail Ahearn and, inspired by her bold aesthetic, she's equally unfazed about using dark, richly pigmented paint, spot color and differences in scale to add drama to a space. As she says admiringly, "Abigail is a master of the dark background with pops of color." The natural light of this little space demanded a warm interior and she played around with eight variations of dark gray paint until she found one that complemented the tone of the cedar wood paneling and fir ceiling beams. She used this to paint the walls and ceiling and thinks this simple treatment

"the best spaces are warm and welcoming while they reflect the interests of the people who live in them . . ."

contributes a whopping 80 percent to the feeling of coziness. The dark gray suits the new purpose of this space, which manages to feel sophisticated yet rustic at the same time.

In terms of the details and the "pops" of color, the red of the fire extinguisher and miniature camp stove inspired the other red accents of the wall lamp and vintage Pendleton wool pillow. Caitlin tried to introduce just enough red without going too far and overdoing it.

Again, influenced by Abigail Ahearn, she likes to use a range of textures in a room. "I try to incorporate a bunch of different textures and sheens into the mix. I like the way the super matte surface of the wood stove and fireproof backing wall look against the rich wood behind them. The table is high gloss and the stump is dry and natural. There isn't much happening by way of pattern, yet there's a lot of texture that the eye picks up."

STYLE NOTES

Caitlin's vision and bold approach to using strong colors and a mixture of contrasting textures makes this warm and inviting space feel stylish yet comfortable and not overfussy. As to her design philosophy, she believes passionately that spaces should be welcoming while reflecting the interests of the people who live in them – above all, they should feel inhabited. She loathes what she describes as "sterile or cookie-cutter spaces" that feel like a catalog. When thinking out the design, she likes to mix different styles and apply her skills and knowledge in a practical, pragmatic way. "I feel I have a pretty good eye for proportions, due to my background in furniture design, so I just wing it and move stuff around until it feels right."

Caitlin wanted to reuse what she already had and avoid spending a lot on new items, so she bought a few lights and a sheepskin from IKEA but repurposed all the older furniture, rugs and art from inside her home. "I painted an old pine work table a glossy black, gathered all the small threadbare carpets I had lying about the house (more than one of which are street finds), framed some art and stole a leather chair from my guest room to finish off the space. The grid of wall studs worked really well for displaying my collection of found objects plus the small *objets d'art* that I've made myself."

The shed is a complete mash-up of high and low design and full of things that have personal significance for Caitlin. The carpets and pillows are vintage, and the wooden stump

15

and crate are street finds, whereas the desk chair is handmade by Thomas Moser and the leather club chair is Restoration Hardware. The surf art is by Andy Davis, but the small photo and print were bought in flea markets. Most of the decorative objects have either been found or made by Caitlin and her son Ethan or they are antiques inherited from her husband's family, including the ship print, bellows and antique weighing devices hanging by the wood stove. Ethan carved the split branch and made the tin can with the triangle cutout, while she created all the wooden cubes and the painting with the red squares.

The front door is Victorian as are the numbers, which were salvaged from the original property. The bell is a family heirloom, originally from a Belgian church, while the yellow buoy was found on the beach at Point Reyes in Northern California, where the family likes to hike every Thanksgiving.

This beautiful space manages to avoid the often slightly depressing assembly of items that usually constitute a "home office." Instead, it's a masterpiece of simplicity, color and texture as well as demonstrating how to use good materials. The appeal of the interior crosses generations within the family, and as a shared space it's hugely successful. Notice the extra-large slate behind the stove, the deluxe finish of the vertical cedar paneling and the relatively luxurious uses and finishes of simple materials. Thoughtful and elegant, they retain the cabin aesthetic, staying in touch with its roots and, consequently, elevating it to something really quite special.

NASHVILLE CAMPER

In a corner of his East Nashville backyard, the writer J. Wes Yoder has created a self-contained short-stay rental apartment in a super-cool vintage Shasta trailer, with a hand-built bathhouse and outdoor shower. When he acquired this legendary beauty of the trailer world she had lost her good looks to beer and squalor, and desperately needed cleaning and rejuvenating, especially the timber bathhouse. For J. Wes, scratching his head, it meant using the know-how he'd gained from watching his Mennonite father and Amish family carry out practical tasks, as well as the old fallback of checking out DIY videos on the web to learn just what to do. As if Nashville weren't already cool enough, the finished "guest room" is fabulously good looking and unassuming. From the get-go, it's been popular with renters and brings J. Wes some additional income.

THE CREATOR

J. Wes wrote his first novel, *Carry My Bones,* in his twenties and since then has worked as a journalist and embarked on his second title. He admires writers like Borges, Calvino, Aira, Vila-Matas and Bolano, whose books feel fresh, light and urgent, giving the impression they were written on the spot. His income comes from the rent generated by his self-created backyard accommodation. He takes a long walk most afternoons and, apart from writing, he loves to cook "kind of as a way of life" and share this passion with his friends, who gather together most nights.

"after a while you just kind of know what you like. You know, you value something because it pleases you in a simple way, not because trends have declared something worthy . . ."

BACKYARD RETREAT

J. Wes grew up south of Nashville in the country. In 2007 he moved back to town, to East Nashville, just across the river from downtown, where he purchased "a little 1920s bungalow and then set about doing projects as and when I had the money to fund them. After I got the backyard closed off and the kitchen opened up onto a deck, I knew that I wanted to put some type of retreat in the corner of the garden. Initially, I thought of a tiny house and drew up the plans and got them approved by the historical commission, but for some reason I wasn't ready to pull the trigger. A friend who was passing through showed me a photo of an old camper she'd bought, and I said: 'That's it.' I liked the lightness of a camper – it took up less space – but I also thought that I could probably tinker my way through the project at an easier pace."

RESTORING THE VINTAGE CAMPER

Vintage trailers, without doubt, have no shortage of charm and beauty. So much so that the reflected glory of a life well lived helps to distract you from the likely horrors that lie hidden in their bodywork, chassis or behind the plywood lining. However, once you've been trapped by their looks, nine times out of ten you are a goner and you're going to buy one regardless, optimistically thinking everything will be OK. J. Wes was no exception. "I found the camper, a '63 Shasta, on eBay the next day. It was 45 minutes away and I went and picked it up. It was a piece of junk and I certainly overpaid, but I've always hated research and digging around. I figured I could make it work."

As it turned out, it was in a really bad way and needed a lot of work. "It was disgusting. It had a lot of water damage, bunk beds, a bathroom that was just a closet with an oil funnel that drained right onto the wheel well. Old blue curtains. And a previous owner who'd had some kind of fetish with Budweiser beer. There was loads of Bud paraphernalia: bottle string lights, signs and a giant Budweiser sticker above the front window. And it was painted red and white, with the typical Shasta lightning bolt paint job."

J. Wes cleaned everything out, including all the junk, until the grim reality was then visible. "The worst was the old water-damaged paneling that flaked into a million pieces, and the 50-year-old dusty insulation that had to be picked out of every nail hole. The place is only 100 sq ft (9.2 sq m), so swinging a crowbar around was really tricky and the whole thing rocked quite a bit. My mom came to see it and was fairly disgusted."

THE PROJECT

J. Wes's plan was to wait tables and pick up writing gigs in order to pay for the renovation gradually on a step-by-step basis. He was "going for broke" because he knew that the camper would work only as a bedroom and that he would have to build the additional bathhouse from scratch, and run plumbing and electricity out to the yard. The day he finished, he had $40 in his account, but in no time at all the bookings started flooding in and he was soon fully booked for the upcoming months.

The cost . . . Well, he didn't really want to think about that too much. "The vision of what it could be was always pleasing and kept me going, even though I don't much enjoy carpentry. The day after I finished I took a long walk. It was crazy how much space I had inside me now that the work was done. For the better part of a year my interior monologue had been mostly lists to take to the Home Depot, screws and cans of caulk and guesses about how much things would cost." It had taken six months of tinkering on the camper – cleaning, painting, rewiring, insulating and then figuring out a way to repanel the interior with thin strips of pine. The bathhouse took another three months to build.

SKILLS

Although J. Wes is the first to admit that his DIY skills are "limited," he was raised in a practical family of very capable people. "My dad's family were Mennonites and his parents grew up Amish. They can build anything. So I picked up a fair amount just growing up around my dad and uncle – how to swing a hammer, use a square and level. But I'm hardly a master carpenter." He also looked online for additional help with specific tasks: "If you're too embarrassed to ask your pops how to use a caulk gun, well, just Google it and some kind Midwesterner's home improvement blog will see you through." Even with his skill set, there were still some things where he just had to find a way to make them work . . . like curtains. "I can't sew, so I bought some cheap linen, cut out the rectangles, left them frayed at the scissor line, and hammered some grommets into the corners. I made curtain rods for the bathhouse out of bamboo donated by a friend, but after all that, the curtains I ordered were ugly, so I ended up hanging Turkish dish towels."

MATERIALS AND PLANNING

Affordability was key. Using primarily pine lumber and "a lot of white paint" he transformed the Shasta. Wanting to create a place with character and charm, and didn't cost the earth, he decided that collected items, if possible, were best. "A friend of mine down in Alabama had the big claw-foot tub sitting out in his woods and gave it to me. It's all beat up but very pretty. And I found a guy to sell me some heart pine flooring; this old growth lumber you can't hardly find anymore. He took it out of an 1820s house they were bulldozing. That's in the bathhouse."

Convention decrees that planning is essential: creating a plan, thinking through the process, being logical, and assessing potential problems are the set approach leading to a successful project. Here, though, free form, courage, practicality and common sense led the way. As J. Wes describes it, "I didn't do a plan for the camper. When the day came to frame the bathhouse I drew a crude picture for my dad and uncle, told them the measurements of the old windows I'd found, and we went from there." Things just worked out, and working backwards from the existing window measurements, the bathhouse, too, was built.

INSTINCTIVE DESIGN

J. Wes's plan was to try and keep things visually simple. The important things to consider were the smallness and agreeable lines of the camper, and how to make the space feel as spacious as possible. He felt that many campers are crowded with too many built-in pieces of furniture and it was more important to "see down into the corners of a space." Accordingly, he replaced the traditional dining benches with chairs and removed the built-in wardrobes, cupboards and drawers. He also kept the color palette simple, believing that in such a small space splashes of color could be added by a vivid blanket, a big orange Dutch oven or just a plant.

"The hardest part of living in Nashville is being eight hours away from any body of salt water. At some point during the project I realized you could view my aesthetic choices as some kind of longing for the coast. I'd gotten rid of the Shasta lighting pattern and painted a sea color around the bottom half. I also wanted the space to feel like the inside of a boat – not that I've been in many boats, but I imagine them looking white and airy, in the canals of Amsterdam perhaps. The camper has a nice curved ceiling and I thought simple white boards would make it kind of nautical."

In terms of the overall aesthetic, J. Wes's approach was highly individualistic, and rather than slavishly following a set look he trusted his own instincts. "I never try for a decorating aesthetic. I just buy things I like and put them together. There are a couple of those Mexican *equipaje* chairs, a small stack of books and a painting a friend made me based on those whale ones that Melville describes in *Moby Dick*, back before any of the artists had ever seen a whale, so they made them look extra mythological." He understands, however, that creating an atmosphere is important, as is having visual props at hand to give clues as to the feel and mood of a place. "There's a little wooden radio that brings in the classical station and a small broadside someone left me of a Gizzi poem, 'In Defense of Nothing.' That's my favorite thing in there."

J. Wes doesn't have a design philosophy: "After a while you just kind of know what you like. You know, you value something because it pleases you in a simple way, not because magazines or trends have declared something worthy. Along the way, my tastes have probably been influenced most by the places I've lived – the Deep South, New Orleans, Oaxaca, Barcelona, New York – and some organic sensitivity towards design elements emerges, a feeling for space, balance, texture, lines and light and all that stuff. Overall my tastes have never been something I wanted to define or figure out too much. But the homes I like the best are the ones that seem they could only belong to the person living there, and I think mine is like that, for better or worse."

THE BACKYARD EXPERIENCE

The attractive bathtub and shower have a peaceful and inviting feel. They have character and make you want to go and have a look, pick up one of the books and laze in the hammock. The outdoor shower has ivy growing around it and when you're in there you just see green and sky. The camper feels private, tucked away and fairly well hidden from the neighborhood. As J. Wes says: "When the trees are in leaf you can't tell it's back there, and from the back of the camper you can hardly see my house, even though it's only 66 ft (20 m) away. It feels very private."

Now that it's finished, the rental is popular. J. Wes has created an experience that is artful, individual, creative, free feeling and an urban adventure. This isn't lost on him or his guests: "The nicest part has been having strangers stay back there. Welcoming them to town and showing them into the garden. There's no TV and no Internet, but they lie in the hammock and shower outside, and a good many people have told me it somehow meant something to stay back there, just the feel of being there, with themselves or with their friend. I remember having those aesthetic experiences when I was young – you know, the kind that make you pay a little more attention to your surroundings, and to have folks respond that way to my little backyard space is a happiness."

STYLE NOTES

Seemingly effortless and without an acknowledged overall vision and plan, this is a wonderfully successful and appealing project. J. Wes is a talented man. Just look at the image of the camper, bathhouse, deck and hammock: each element is set in such a way that it relates to the others. The deck has been built so that everything is on the same level, creating a comfortable whole environment for guests. The front edge is appealingly softly curved where it meets the rest of the garden.

Internally the camper has been stripped clean and treated as if it's a bedroom. It has the wonderful Shasta design, horizontally striated exterior, curved shape and louvered windows, while the white-painted horizontal interior pine cladding mirrors the exterior. It's a whole. It's the same with the bathhouse, which is painted white and similarly lined with white horizontal pine boards. It echoes the Shasta and is a complete space with its own environment. The sloping roof and additional windows in the eaves have created a wonderfully bright interior, and the genuinely aged rolltop bath adds the vintage texture that pulls it all together. Inexpensive, beautiful, and a unique means of creating a rental income in your own backyard, this really is supercool.

BEN'S GARDEN WORKSHOP

What must be one of the most precise and perfect backyard workshop sheds ever, this is a wonderful example of precision and good design springing from a sound and meaningful inspiration. It's based on the proportions of the owner's grandfather's old woodworking bench, and the handcrafted tools that decorate the walls also play their part in the "story" of this remarkable building. The simplicity is elegant, the precision considered, the ordinary is elevated, and the shed's functional qualities have become beautiful. Read on . . .

THE OWNER
Ben Davidson is an architect working in the London-based studio of Rodic Davidson. He lists his passions as making things, taking things apart and putting them back together again. Practicality is key to his design philosophy: he always wants to be able to build anything he designs himself although he rarely has the time.

MODEL-MAKING WORKSHOP
This simple timber-framed building is one of two sheds located at the end of Ben's long back garden at his home in Cambridge, England. One is a home office while this structure functions as a model-making workshop. The proportions are those of his grandfather's old workbench, and the fine-crafted tools are hung on pegboard walls. The shed was designed around the size of the workbench and a number of large glazed panels that had been given to Ben by a contractor several years earlier. The workshop is such a success that it has become a prototype for subsequent buildings that the practice has designed for its clients.

FINDING INSPIRATION
The main inspiration for this unique project was Ben's grandfather, an extraordinarily talented carpenter who handmade most of the beautiful tools that are on display. The workshop celebrates his collection of tools and great care has been taken in their arrangement. As Ben says: "It's a gallery, really. I remember many happy summers back in my early teens when I stayed with my grandparents in Norfolk and spent the entire time with my grandfather in his workshop."

BEN'S PLAN

Ben knew what he wanted to achieve and had a vision in his mind early on, but it was the big picture rather than the sum of all the details. To the "mild frustration" of the builders, he designed this building as the detail emerged and the project progressed. Every morning before leaving for work, he would set things out that he wanted done that day.

In his own words: "I communicated my vision and, more practically, I paid the builders on a day rate (as opposed to a fixed sum). I believe this was critical to the quality of the outcome. I needed the flexibility to make design decisions as the project evolved, and I wanted the builders to focus on quality rather than time. A fixed-sum contract could only have worked with a fully detailed scheme of drawings and schedule – something I didn't want to do. I wanted hands-on engagement and a design process that enabled ad hoc collaborative contributions from the craftsmen who were doing the construction." This was really important to Ben. He wanted to avoid the usual separation between "architect" and "contractor," and for the craftsmen to influence his detailed design decisions. By working in this way, he could better understand what the builders were best at doing and utilize these specific skills. He saw his role in the project as leading and communicating, not "telling" them what to do.

MATERIALS AND BUILD

Ben decided to use inexpensive, readily available materials, including timber, glass, concrete and ply, to create a workshop that would be modest yet contemporary. His choice of birch plywood and tanalized timber met his criteria for honesty and simplicity. Outside, the shed is clad with vertical black-stained softwood boards that are laid over a waterproof rubber membrane wrapper. Inside, the stud work is constructed out of 6 x 2 softwood. Ben used a concrete base for the floor and ground it for the terrazzo – a composite material that is used for wall and floor treatments. As well as the large windows set into the side walls, two overhead skylights help to flood the interior space with light.

An exposed wooden box frame fits around the old wooden workbench that Ben inherited from his talented craftsman grandfather. Pieces of pegboard lined with hooks fill the square recesses sitting within the frame. They were all cut specially to fit and then sprayed with seven coats of satin lacquer. Suspended from the hooks are the exquisitely crafted tools, some of which Ben, as a boy, helped his grandfather to make.

STYLE NOTES

Although this is a tidy, workmanlike space, it also feels friendly and cozy with a strong aesthetic. Everything has its own designated place and is neatly stowed away in modular wooden shelving boxes and birch ply cupboards, while many of the tools hang in a predetermined logical order from the exposed hooks, bestowing a gallery-type atmosphere. In addition to Ben's grandfather's workbench, there's another maple workbench running along one wall beneath a large window and incorporating a lower platform for a pillar drill and a sink.

Despite all the tools and specialist items of equipment, it would be easy and pleasurable to work in this quiet and tranquil place. Every object has an equal value and is displayed to its best advantage. Even the color palette has been carefully considered – it's refreshingly neutral throughout, making it easy on the eye, with no surprising splashes of bold colors. White, gray and shades of brown predominate inside, broken up only by the odd blue machine.

ANDERSON SHED

Created for a family in Seattle, this practical, attractive backyard storage space serves as a modern architectural reinvention of the classic garden potting shed. Only too often, an effective garden repository means a hidden-away ramshackle building stuffed to the gills with out-of-season items you don't know what to do with. However, here the Seattle-based SHED Architecture & Design practice has created a means of garden storage that is both practical and beautiful.

THE BACKGROUND

The commission to remodel the back garden of a midcentury house looked at the whole design of the exterior space. The house had no obvious storage areas, such as a basement or garage, and the only place to create additional storage space was within the back garden. However, planning restrictions did not permit any building too near the rear perimeter fence, so the design needed to be within the garden area itself and have a visual presence to warrant a prime position within the backyard.

DESIGN BRIEF

The design brief from the client was to provide more storage for bicycles and garden equipment within the whole garden scheme as well as a potting shed area with enough space to store gardening materials. In addition, this was a place where the owners could work and tend the plants. It was designed as an S-shaped structure with two faces of color to make it fun to interact with. Key to the architect Prentice's design philosophy were simplicity, how the structure blends with the rest of the garden and the visual balance the building needed to achieve – enough to warrant its position but not so much that it overwhelmed the space as a whole. The building was given a green roof to help it meld seamlessly into the garden when it was viewed from above.

MATERIALS

Using a steel structure that has a mild surface rust finish added a richer color and character to the building. The wood cladding is Brazilian cherry, a hardwood that is very resistant to decay, grays with age and needs no rot protection. The cladding was definitely part of the overall look and feel of the shed in its space in such a prime location in the yard. The walls and cladding were designed to blend with the existing fencing in the garden.

STYLE NOTES

Echoing an angular midcentury architectural pavilion, this simply shaped functional garden storage shed has acquired an elegance. The steel beams that shoot out from the building expand its presence in the garden and help to soften the potential for the exterior of the shed to look severe or to end abruptly visually. The material choice helps the shed contextually to fit in with the rest of the garden.

Designing the walls in horizontal slats, with a regular spaced gap between them, prevents the structure from appearing too heavy. The opening and closing of the different sections, with the doors sliding open, means that it feels more like a building you interact with rather than simply enter. It has a surprising lightness of touch, almost the feel of a magic box that opens up via secret compartments.

The interior of the shed, although it's used for storage, echoes that spirit. Painted with leftover paint from decorating the children's bedrooms, the potting shed on one side is a bright blue; the bike and kayak storage on the other side, pink. Over time the external tonal palette will naturally evolve with the weathering of the steel and the cherrywood, gaining a grayish hue and blending into the surrounding garden.

The interior sections are painted with leftover paint from the house. This adds an energy, a surprising counterpoint to the regular form of the cherrywood and steel exterior.

When the sliding doors are closed, the steel surround on which they run frames the view looking back towards the house and also creates a visual link, which helps to soften the abruptness of the building within the garden itself.

HAND-BUILT GREENHOUSE

Jerry Reddy is the quintessential Canadian outdoors man. A retired telephone engineer, he has a deep passion for nature, not only in its most epic form but also its smallest details. He is especially interested in geology, conservation and living an environmentally sensitive life. Originally from Ontario, he was raised in a family with an outdoor practical lifestyle; they went wild camping, setting off with just a backpack and making impromptu shelters as they went along. Now living with his wife on a 64-acre (30-ha) estate in the maritime climate of Nova Scotia, Jerry has had to adapt to deal with a windswept cooler location and to grow the vegetables they enjoyed in Ontario. To achieve this he built himself a greenhouse. What's so unusual about that? . . . Well, read on.

A SELF-SUFFICIENT LIFESTYLE

The couple live in the most self-sufficient way possible, growing as much of their food as they can, using organic principles and heritage seeds. They cultivate tomatoes, peppers and cucumbers, and each season they collect and store the seeds, ready to plant again the following year. At this period of his life, Jerry has found a richness and developed a different approach and purpose: "My philosophy in life has changed as I age, and now into my sixties I am more concerned with permanency than looks. I want the things that I build to last for a very long time. Here I am in northern Nova Scotia, living a very different life to the one I had in Ontario. I work alone most of the time and I've adopted the mindset that you must rely solely on yourself to achieve your goals, much the same as the early pioneers would have done. Self-reliance and hard work are the order of my life."

THE GEOGRAPHY

Over the years the land use of the estate had gradually changed. Once heavily wooded, the land had been cleared for grazing for livestock and modern large-scale agricultural practices. Unlike Ontario, the weather here in Nova Scotia is wild, windy, stormy and cold.

SOURCING THE MATERIALS

Because of the prevailing weather conditions, the remote location and the couple's environmental principles, it was important to them that the materials selected for building the greenhouse were locally sourced, robust, and reclaimed or recycled as much as possible. The plan gained momentum when a supply of old windows became available to Jerry and he set about sourcing the materials for building the foundations. The structure had to be substantial, so he needed to construct it to last as long as possible.

When the surrounding woodland was originally cleared to make it into farmland, large stones from the land were collected into huge piles and Jerry used these for the foundations. The stones needed cleaning in order to create a surface that would allow the mortar to bond, so using muriatic acid, Jerry meticulously cleaned the organic matter off every stone to create a bondable finish. For mortar he used 100 five-gallon buckets of sand from the nearby beach, mixed with cement powder. Over a three-month backbreaking period of intensive labor, the foundations of the greenhouse were laid.

As much timber as possible came from the family's wood lot, consisting only of the wood from dead trees cut into lumber. The wooden-framed, oblong-paned windows were sourced from a neighbor's house, which was built in the 1800s and was having a makeover. Jerry asked if he could have the old ones that were being removed but then discovered he was second in line. The windows had been donated to the local historic society, but when they didn't turn up to collect them they found a caring home with Jerry instead. For roofing materials he sourced some galvanized steel from an old abandoned barn and, using as many reclaimed materials as possible, he only needed to purchase some wood to build the structure at the back of the greenhouse.

> "keep it as simple and as near to the old ways as possible and think in terms of how the early pioneers would have done things before we had everything we do today . . ."

JERRY'S PHILOSOPHY AND INSPIRATION

Jerry's essential philosophy in life is "to keep everything as simple and as near to the old ways as possible and to think in terms of how the early pioneers would have done things before we had everything we do today. And my inspirations for the greenhouse . . . bacon and tomato sandwiches, fresh salads and dill pickles!"

SKILLS

Jerry has always been a self-taught and very practical man, learning many of his skills when he was a child watching other members of his family at work, as well as through trial and error helping to build cabins and go-carts in the 1950s and '60s. Later on in life when he bought his own house, he purchased a copy of the *Reader's Digest DIY Manual*, and from that source he learned everything else he needed to know.

STYLE NOTES

As soon as the building was finished, Jerry and his wife gathered an eclectic assortment of things they liked from the surrounding area and put them on the shelves in the greenhouse. "We found a poor owl that had met his end somehow and there he rests on a shelf with a beaver as a neighbor. We always marvel at the intricate weaves of birds' nests and how perfectly shaped they are, even after they have reared their young, so we added these, too."

In keeping with the recycled nature of this project, everything they collected and displayed inside the greenhouse has had a previous use. The different-colored old glass bottles were dug up from a garbage dump and displayed against the window panes: "The colors of the glass bottles catch the sunshine and give us a ray of hope for a good harvest in the fall." The cattle skull comes from the period when the land was used for grazing, and their huge respect for the natural world means that items such as crows' and rooks' nests, bones and birds' feathers, all found around the property, have each been given their special place. Preserved and displayed in all their different shapes and styles, each nest provides an illustration of the creativity of the birds that collected the different materials and constructed them.

Jerry left any original paint on the wooden windows rather than strip them "so that the greenhouse would look as if it had been there for many years. The colors blend into our northern skies that are so often gray, filled with snow and rain."

Decorating a practical space requires careful thought. Here, using found objects from the land, still life vignettes have been created that represent the area and the previous uses of the land. The items and the effect of their collection and grouping is beautiful, genuine and relevant.

CINEMA STUDIO SHED

In a conservation area of Georgian properties in Hackney, East London, this back garden studio is a strikingly architectural and graphic-shaped building that serves the different needs of the owners, a video artist and an art theoretician. It has many uses, including a video projection space, a bright work studio, a darkroom for film developing and an area for working on sculptures. It had to be a fun place for the children, too – and all of this set within a restricted 215 sq ft (20 sq m) footprint.

THE BRIEF

For Krishan Pattni, an architect and creative director of the London-based practice Latis, the challenge was to create in a positive way "the impossible garden shed," which worked within planning legislation and complied with the complex usage needs without digging up too much of the garden. He wanted to design "an object full of surprise that provided an unexpected experience of the context, and had to be fun for the children." Because of its conservation area location, erecting a studio needed planning permission, and a key planning strategy was to minimize the impact of the volume of the building, creating a two-story interior within a single-story exterior.

SPACE AND LIGHT

The challenge was not only how to create the specific volumes and heights required within the space, while keeping within the limited footprint and permitted building height, but also not to lose too much of the usable garden space itself. The architects found a workable and beautiful solution. By creating height by digging downwards and installing a half basement to use as the principal level in the shed, the height and space requirements could be achieved. The additional height created allowed for a mezzanine floor to become a secondary space, thereby providing a light, bright area above, and a dark space below. Two large angled roof lights are the principal source of top light within the building, along with the huge 25 sq ft (2.4 sq m) square glazed wall at the front.

OUTWARDS AND INWARDS

In any city back garden, the design, structures, fences and landscaping of the neighbors' gardens impact on you. You look downwards and outwards

from the upper floors, and laterally, too, not only in terms of light and landscape but also garden builds. Here, the exterior shape and tones of this visually striking structure sited between the neighbors' builds make it feel and look dynamic – it has an energy all its own.

Internally, it's a forward-looking building, facing the back of the tall Georgian house. Similarly, within the shed the different floor heights have created various sight lines and framed views backwards through the garden. The huge square window has a visual dialog, a relationship with the imposing large living room window of the main house, and at night things are reversed. The darkened studio window becomes a reverse-projection cinema screen for private viewings in the garden.

SUSTAINABILITY AND MATERIALS

Sustainability within a limited budget was achieved by cleverly utilizing conventional recycled materials in an innovative way. FSC- (Forest Stewardship Council)-certified timber was used for the main structure, which was then covered in recycled impregnated corrugated sheet cladding reminiscent of more rural sheds. This black exterior material has a canvas-like surface texture and an undulating, corrugated form onto which the light falls, thereby creating areas of darker and lighter tones.

Internally the walls are painted white to create a contrast with the dark exterior, while a decision was made to deliberately leave the interior floorings exposed in structural concrete and timber. The large glazed window wall acts to illuminate the interior and is also important for its reflective qualities, picking up the reflections of the nearby trees and foliage along with the cinematic projections.

In this shed, which is cinematic in its style and function, the sharp and strong architectural form of the building itself informs the surface finish on the interior. The two interior design parameters are the contained color palette and strong tonal range between black and white, and the large panes of glass and light plywood.

STYLE NOTES

With its origami-like angular form and black, white and glass palette, this unusual structure is a striking piece of architecture – a place that is equally good to look at and to be in. Its essential angular form is repeated in the smaller details of the building. For instance, the angle of the top of the front door echoes the one on the slope of the building directly above it as well as the angular roof lights.

The half basement area and desk space have windows at eye level looking back across the garden towards the house. Open-tread stairs link the semibasement with the upper level. This place is all about levels, angles, eyelines, unexpected views, window openings that open and close, and spaces that can be used in changing and different ways. It really is a folding magic box of a building.

With such strong architecture it's best just to leave it to speak clearly, and not overcomplicate things with too many interior details. It's better without curtains or window treatments, without too much furniture and stuff. It's a place that manages to conjure up a clever equilibrium between all the different elements and facilitates creativity while enabling that essential companion of concentration on the task at hand. The balance of inwards and outwards is encouraged and just about perfect.

ARTIST'S POOL HOOSE

An artist, shed builder and long-distance cyclist, Peter McClaren paints in oil on large canvases and has won numerous prestigious awards, but he also likes to work in wood, constructing individual sheds with primarily found materials. "I'm a serial cabin, folly and woodpile builder. I've restored an Orcadian croft, Edinburgh New Town apartments and Victorian conservatories. I've also rebuilt a vintage car and tractor." From his early years he appreciated the wider creative possibilities of wood: "When I was a child my mum gave me a saw, some board and planks, a set square and a measuring tape. It was the best thing that ever happened to me. I made a coffee table that fell down immediately, but the seed was planted."

ADAPTABILITY AND INFLUENCES

For Peter, the adaptable and free-form, organic nature of self-building is uniquely special. "I'm a painter, so I have to be able to respond to changes as things develop. I'm different from an architect, who is bound by convention and all the regulations. I wouldn't do it if I was confined to those limitations. An artist really has free rein."

He travels, preferably by bicycle, and what he sees on the road informs both his paintings and his shed building: "I go to stay with my sister in France by bike. You see things on a bike that you would never notice otherwise, and you're more inclined to stop, take pictures and speak to folk. I get inspiration from seeing things online as well." France is a relatively short journey for Peter. In 2011, he rode his bicycle on a mammoth 4,300-mile (6,920-km) journey across America, stopping at public libraries along the way to use their Wi-Fi to update his online journal, send e-mails and gain local knowledge. One day, delayed en route by a heavy thunderstorm, he took shelter in a library to wait for the weather to pass and one of the patrons offered him the use of her cabin in nearby Alma, only a short distance down the road – this proved to be a significant encounter that was to inform one of Peter's builds.

THE LOCATION

For the last 40 years, Peter's extended family has lived in a large property in Scotland. The grounds are extensive but not entirely user- or viewer-friendly. The "problem" with the walled garden is that once you're in, you can't see out, and when you're out, you can't see in. However, a vantage point on a nearby hilltop afforded a good view of the garden, enclosed by a very high wall, so Peter decided to find a way of building some outbuildings that would create a higher vantage point within the garden itself to enable the family to see outwards, too. Once the initial outbuilding had been built, there was the capability and space for another, and the construction work continued all around the garden.

Structures in which a large proportion of the surface area is glass can create a slightly uncomfortable, exposed feeling for the occupant. Here the large amount of glass is balanced by the surrounding tree branches, foliage and natural wood texture of the floor and interior ceiling. Texture, warmth and comfort are added by the choice of upholstered furniture, blankets and softly lit large table lamps.

MATERIALS

Reusing materials is Peter's preference, and their size and qualities often inform the ultimate design of a shed. For the construction of the Pool Hoose he used entirely recycled materials, including telegraph poles, scaffolding battens, timber, roofing tin and glass. "The old telegraph poles were great when they were free and I used some of my best ones to build Doric temples. The telephone company used to give them away until a European Union directive banned the practice because they are pressure-treated with carcinogenic creosote. I reflected on my 'squandering' a dozen of my best poles on a Doric folly elsewhere in the garden."

In fact, the sourcing of the materials, the excitement and the creative, motley selection of items are a driver towards Peter's building: "If I had to go to a builders' merchants and buy all the stuff, I would never do it. There's no thrill in that. For me, it's all about the fun of discovering something and then finding a new life for it. I think the telegraph poles are special when they're painted white. I just want to hug them."

THE POOL HOOSE

Peter's idea was to build an elevated structure, with views over and into the garden – a haven and secret hideaway for lazy afternoons. Many years earlier, at his mother's suggestion, he had dug out a pool in the walled garden "as a character-building initiative." Between the pool and the 8 ft (2.4 m) high wall a rambling rose had become wildly overgrown, and when it was cut back a space was revealed where a monkey puzzle tree and a spruce were planted. He decided to build a summerhouse with a floor level at 8 ft (2.4 m), so he could see both pools and into the walled garden. To achieve this, he would recycle a pile of salvaged scaffolding boards and some old tin roofing. "With no real plan other than a back-of-an-envelope sketch, which was really more of a wish list, the style was Chinese pavilion meets Vietnamese boathouse."

Peter wanted a covered walkway under the eaves around the perimeter of the building, so he started digging. "I dug holes for the six poles to a depth of between 3 ft (0.9 m) and 4 ft (1.2 m), approximately the same as would be needed to support a telephone line. By suppertime we had them in place and the makings of a deck floor laid. The following day I made some trusses for the roof and we hauled them up. With the recycled roofing in place, it started to look like something that might work."

"with no real plan other than a back-of-an-envelope sketch, which was really more of a wish list, the style of this tree house was Chinese pavilion meets Vietnamese boathouse . . ."

Peter used scaffolding boards for the floor to add to stability, but his plans for the building's shape changed, and by extending the side walls outwards and sacrificing the walkway he made the interior more spacious.

He didn't feel his stash of old Georgian sash windows would be suitable – he wanted larger paned windows. A few months before he had noticed a local house renovation with a pile of glass from a dismantled conservatory stacked against an outbuilding. When he drove over to investigate, to his relief, it was still there. Pure serendipity! He could have it for free if he took it away right then. The side walls were constructed with specific openings to accommodate the salvaged windows.

Peter furnished the summerhouse in keeping with its "lazy afternoon hideaway" status. When a friend told him he was participating in a day without electricity experiment, he was intrigued. He did a sleepover in his new shed and enjoyed it so much he spent some of the following winter and spring sleeping there. "It swayed like a tree house in the fiercest storms, and the monkey puzzle scratched the tin roof like a determined axe murderer. But even a pheasant sliding off the roof in the snow or an early morning bird strike on the glass seldom disturbed my sleep."

The following summer Peter was back on his bike on a cycle tour of Oregon. Caught out in torrential rain, he remembered he had registered as a Warm Showers host. It's an organization run by touring cyclists where hosts offer either a bed or a spot on which to pitch your tent plus a supper and a hot bath or shower. He called a host and stayed with them not just for the night but, as the forecast was bad, for the following day, too. It turned out to be the best couple of days in his two-month tour, and when he got back home to Scotland he thought of offering the Pool Hoose to fellow traveling cyclists and set about furnishing the shed for overnight visitors. He has now hosted riders from Canada, Germany, Argentina, America and China. Happy that the Pool Hoose was never conceived as anything but a modest cabin with a view, he is pleased that it has been so well received.

THE TREE HOUSE EXPERIENCE

With the feeling of being in a tree house, you get a sense of the elements. "The full force of the morning sun wakes you up. It's like being in a greenhouse. And it's nice when it rains – there's this tremendous pitter-patter on the roof. It's even great in a storm when you get a bit of a sway. It's not for the faint hearted." The green curtain of the foliage outside reinforces the tree house feeling as well as creating some privacy. Peter sums it up well: "The thing that gets you when you're up here is the light. When you're in the garden you are really enclosed and feel as though you are crawling through the jungle. It's fun to be up here among the trees."

CONTEMPLATIVE

Sheds can be contemplative and thoughtful spaces as well as busy working ones. All these sheds were designed to be meditative places where you can sit and think, be inspired or just dream. These quiet spaces nurture creativity and are perfect for artistic folk. Many of them are located in remote and beautiful landscapes where you can retreat from the bustle of everyday life and engage with nature. What links them all is their creators' commitment to a strong design ethos and their capacity to inspire us to creative endeavor.

On a Swedish island some designers have collaborated to create a waxed cotton A-frame tent for an annual international design festival under canvas. At the end, it can be packed up and stand, totem-like, in the landscape until the following year's festivities. On the edge of a cliff overlooking the sea in Norfolk, England, stands an extraordinary tower used by its owner, Pete, as a retreat. The side walls can be raised by a pulley mechanism to create an open-sided pavilion where on warm nights you can sleep outside under a canopy of stars.

Bothies were traditionally remote small huts or cottages in mountainous areas used as shelters by local workers, but The Bothy Project has given them a contemporary edge and a new look. Three of these innovative remote buildings are featured: an eco-friendly artist's residence in the Hebrides, an off-grid cabin on the banks of the Spey in Cairngorms National Park and a sustainable timber-clad shed in the grounds of the Scottish National Gallery of Modern Art in Edinburgh. They are all part of a wider plan to create a network of residency spaces that inspire artists to explore Scotland's unique landscape and mythology.

Romance and fantasy play their part, too. Two whimsical cabins facing each other across a lake in rural Northumberland are the physical manifestations of a fairy-tale romance between two imaginary characters. In this instance, a narrative has been used to create a special place where walkers and cyclists can pause and stare. Deep in rural England is another romantic and unusual building inspired by the shape of a pigeon's breast. However, this charming folly, which takes its references from the natural world, is also a practical shelter. Far away on the shore of a Canadian lake stands a different type of folly. Carraig Ridge is a witty and modern take on a traditional fireplace, which serves as a social space.

FREYA & ROBIN

In rural Northumberland two small cabins sit on either side of a lake. Their forms are simple but considered, and although they are specific to this site, what's of particular interest is their design and the way in which materials, techniques and finishes have been utilized to create a brief in the form of a narrative that "ties" the two together. Delicate and beautiful, these simple cabins function as shelters for walkers and cyclists.

ORIGINS

The cabins were commissioned as part of the Kielder Art and Architecture Program. The objective was to develop one or more structures on the bank of Kielder Water to provide a stopping place for visitors out walking or cycling along the lakeside path. They would also provide visible markers or destination points from which to begin or end a walk or a bike ride. Kielder is home to the largest man-made body of water in Europe and surrounded by commercial forest. The two cabins, named "Freya" and "Robin," are the result of this commission.

A FAIRY TALE

Studio Weave, which also designed Ecology of Color (see page 168), took on the commission. Their approach is to work within the context and local environment to create a narrative through which a project can become real and the two can merge to become one. In this case they began by embracing the man-made nature of the "rural" landscape and considering the site as a stage or backdrop against which they could tell a story.

Two sites were chosen, one on each side of Kielder Water and Forest Park, and the story woven was an imagined fairy tale of two characters, Freya and Robin. The two cabins were to be physical manifestations of the love story, connected by a magical link across the water that separates them. The structures form stopping points that gaze at each other and enhance a sense of place along the new Lakeside Way.

Studio Weave describes the purpose of this story tale approach: "We developed a narrative that guided and informed our design decisions from beginning to end, proving an effective forum in which the architect, client and fabricator could collaborate. While creating evidence of an imagined fairy tale, the pavilions also meet technically demanding requirements, including all-year-round accessibility, robustness for constant public use and resistance to extreme weather conditions."

→Freya, the more decorative of the two cabins, has a copper-hued exterior that richly glows in the sunlight. It's clad in an alloy of copper, aluminum and zinc, and with delicately twisting tree-branch end panels cut from spruce.

↓Robin is the simpler of this pair of cabins, open ended and clad in cedar or larch shingles. Their rooflines mirror each other on opposite sides of the lake.

THE STORY

The story features two characters who live opposite each other across the water: Robin in a simple wooden hut situated on the edge of the forest on the north bank of the lake, and Freya, who loves flowers (and Robin, too!), on the south bank. Freya expresses her romantic feelings for Robin by making him the gift of an intricate cabin in the image of the woodland he loves so much.

Meanwhile, over the water, he's building a boat, which Freya interprets as his desire to row across to her and the cabin. However, because the cabin is on the south bank, Robin can't see it, nor Freya, due to the sun shining in his eyes, and really he is planning to go off on an adventure.

Once Freya realizes that Robin is rowing in the opposite direction, she is so upset that she cries tears of real gold. As she lovingly wraps the cabin in her golden tears, Robin sees something glinting in the distance and rows across the water towards it. He is so moved by the cabin that he invites Freya to accompany him on his adventure. They didn't leave very long ago, so they are still away adventuring, but you can see Robin's wooden hut and the golden cabin that Freya made for him, facing each other across the lake, awaiting their return.

47

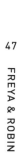

FREYA & ROBIN

MATERIALS

In the story Freya models the cabin on her flower press, taking tree branches and pressing them tightly together to create an enchanted forest ceiling, then balancing it up high on the tallest, straightest stems she can find. This fantasy design is echoed in the real construction of her cabin, which is made from spruce plywood panels chosen for their prominent grain and economy of use. The panels were CNC (computer numeric control) cut, and more than 1,600 individual pieces were assembled in the form of a puzzle book to create the cabin. Birdsmouth joints were included in the cutting drawings to ease the assembly.

The little cabin moves significantly, depending on the water content of the timber. The use of glue has been minimized to ensure that the panels can breathe and dry out as naturally as possible. The layers are held together with 10 steel rods sprung at each end to maintain tension as the cabin expands and contracts throughout the year. The spruce panels were individually treated with a water-repellent organic oil that cuts out UV light and protects against scratching. The plywood is interspersed with clear acrylic sheets, which admit the light and form the balustrade. The structure is held up on lots of brass-clad metal "stems" planted into concrete foundations. Preformed trays of Luvata's Nordic Royal, an alloy of copper, with aluminum and zinc to maintain their golden shade, were used as Freya's golden tears to wrap the cabin. The copper-aluminum sheets were chosen for their warm and lasting golden finish. They were perforated in a tear-like pattern and fixed so as to allow movement as the structure breathes with the ever-changing weather.

DESIGN PHILOSOPHY

The cabin that Freya built for Robin is in the image of what she imagines his woodland home to be like. For the walls she arranged the strongest branches, working from thick to thin. And for the roof she made an enchanted forest ceiling with twisted branches tickling each other and plenty of round green apples that she knew were Robin's favorite. She put foxgloves at the entrance to invite the fairies in, then pressed everything tightly together, so they would stay strong and crisp and last forever.

In contrast, Robin's hut is a simple wooden structure clad in larch or cedar shingles. It has the same pitched-roof profile as Freya's cabin and the two buildings line up and face each other across the stretch of water. Sited among fir trees and rocks, it's surrounded by water, giving it a remote, island-like feel. Robin wanted to live beside the woods, where he loves to climb trees and play with the animals.

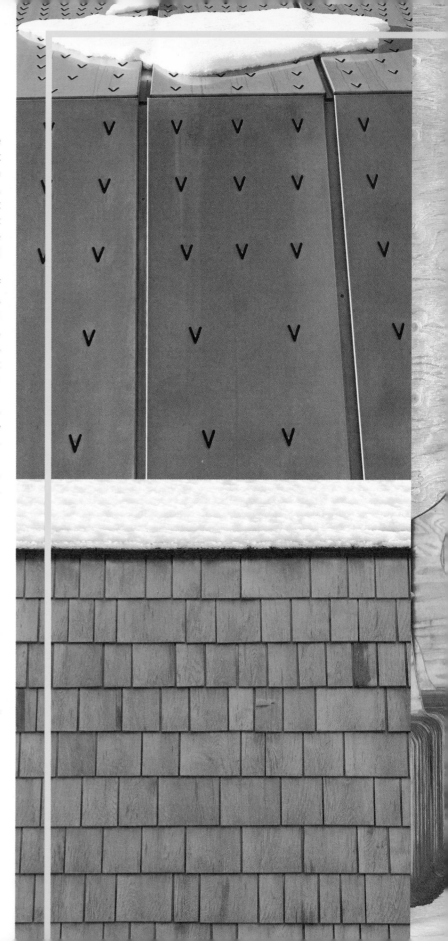

STYLE NOTES

Studio Weave are masters at using the form of a narrative to create individual, inventive and creative structures. And rather than seeing finishes as a simple decorative practical treatment on the exterior, they combine the materials, the form of the building and the finish to create the magical wholeness. These little cabins are inspired. We often talk about inside out, how to connect two different spaces, the separate elements of a design and how we use a space. Here's a stunning example of one beautiful whole. This unique approach, albeit undoubtedly whimsical, has proved to be an incredibly useful working tool in creating a wonderful and magical space.

The aspect from Freya's cabin is one of a long wistful gaze across the water, and the exquisite detail and delicacy of the cabin structure engage your eye and create a space that's comfortable, where you want to linger.

PIG ROCK BOTHY

This project was sponsored by the stove manufacturer Esse and Russwood, Scotland's leading supplier of high-quality, sustainable timber products. To design and handcraft it, a highly creative team from The Bothy Project, including the artists Bobby Niven and Will Foster and the architect Iain MacLeod, worked in collaboration with Douglas Flett Architects and the Glasgow-based artist Laura Aldridge.

THE BOTHY PROJECT

This unique structure stands within the grounds of Modern One at the Scottish National Gallery of Modern Art in Edinburgh. It was commissioned to provide a temporary venue for a dynamic and changing program of residencies, discussions, performances and events as part of the 2014 Generation exhibition, which celebrates 25 years of contemporary art in Scotland. Traditionally, bothies are small huts providing basic shelter and refuge, especially in wild, mountainous terrains.

THE DESIGN

The inspiration for the bothy was the wild and windswept environment of its future home in the Scottish Highlands. The design was based on giving a playful twist to the concept of a bold, vernacular form, and the structure slants outwards, as if it's being blown over by persistent high winds.

INSPIRATION

This bothy was created as part of The Bothy Project's wider plan to construct a network of artists' residency spaces in diverse locations around Scotland with the objective of exploring the country's unique mythology, landscape and people. The project is committed to designing small-scale dwellings for hosting visual artists, writers and musicians who want to experiment with renewable energy systems and the challenges of living off-grid. The idea behind the project is to inspire artists to conceive innovative ideas and create new work by providing them with platforms for living within remote and beautiful landscapes.

The original plan of relocating this building to a permanent site at Assynt in northwest Scotland, where it would become the third bothy in the art residency network, was shelved when the Scottish National Galleries decided to build a separate bothy there and to twin the two structures, connecting the two sites' communities, activities and environments.

The Bothy Project is committed to sustainable materials and building techniques, and this structure is no exception. The timber frame incorporated larch, Douglas fir and oak, with an outer cladding of polycarbonate.

Designed at an angle to represent the blast from the strong winds at its eventual location in the Scottish Highlands, the Pig Rock Bothy is not only an inviting shelter but also an inspiration, a retreat and an artist's functional workspace.

STYLE NOTES

This little space's eccentric name was coined by the artist Laura Aldridge, who was commissioned to create a body of work to furnish it. As part of her research she visited Assynt – the proposed final resting place for the bothy – to get a feel for the landscape. She was inspired by the pink and gray lichen-spotted rocks there that resembled a pig's skin. Laura translated the organic patterns and colors of the natural environment onto the surfaces of her fabrics, textiles and ceramics, which help to define and adorn this special space.

One of the resident artists, Victoria Evan, describes it as an "inside/outside" space. It has a unique quality of stillness that fosters contemplation and inner reflection. Victoria set up in a comfortable corner of the bothy and invited visitors to come and be drawn while chatting about their experiences of galleries, contemporary art and what it feels like to sit for a portrait. "And on one or two wonderful occasions both the sitter and I relaxed into the encounter and the drawing and interaction came together, resulting in a sketch that became the likeness not just of a person but of an experience." And thereby the function of this translucent structure was to spotlight the essential process of making art.

INSHRIACH BOTHY

Like the other two bothies featured in this book, the Inshriach Bothy was designed by The Bothy Project as a modern off-grid living and working space for artist residencies. It, too, is located away from the bustle of modern digitized life in a rustic setting to encourage creativity and the imaginative process. The first bothy to be built, it's the branchild of architectural designer Iain MacLeod and artist Bobby Niven.

STRUCTURE AND PURPOSE

Built off-site at the Edinburgh Sculpture Workshop, this bothy was transported by road to its current location on the Inshriach Estate, where it sits on the banks of the River Spey in a wooded area of the Cairngorms National Park near Aviemore. In addition to the living space and mezzanine bedroom area, there's a working studio space, which is perfect for painting, drawing, small-scale sculptural work, bricolage, wood carving or just reading and contemplation.

A PIONEERING IDEA

This is a pioneering project where art meets tourism. Inspired by the desire to create a lasting legacy of small-scale ongoing residency spaces for artists, The Bothy Project is doing something that is truly innovative. To fund the costs of running the bothy and to make it available for artists, it is rented out as a holiday venue for paying guests for part of the year.

THE DESIGN

True to the principles of the project, this little cabin in the pine and birch woods was designed around some recycled sash windows from Bobby Niven's Glasgow apartment and a ladder that was found in a dumpster outside the Glasgow School of Art. The plan was to create something custom-made and interesting but also unfussy so as not to impose too much of an aesthetic on the visiting artists who use the bothy, and it has succeeded.

MATERIALS AND BUILD

Sandwiched between the external cladding of wood and corrugated iron and the internal wooden frame is a thick layer of sheep's wool insulation. The floor is fashioned out of reclaimed wooden planks. Built and assembled on-site over a six-month period by volunteers from the Edinburgh Sculpture Workshop, this structure is disarmingly simple.

STYLE NOTES

This bothy might be off-grid and off the beaten track, but it's well insulated, warm and inviting. Cozy and comfortable, it has an environmentally friendly solar panel lighting system and phone charger and a solar windup radio and torch. A wood-burning stove heats the space as well as the hot water for the outside suspended bag shower – and it even has an oven for cooking your meals. So although it's a real back-to-nature experience, the visiting artists and paying guests can still enjoy some of life's little luxuries.

This is the ultimate back-to-basics space and it appeals to anyone who's ever been afflicted with "cabin fever" and yearns to escape to the wilderness. Sitting by a crackling real log fire on a cold night with a saucepan of stew gently simmering away on the stovetop and filling the space with its savory aroma, while the wind moans in the surrounding trees, is a remarkably contemplative experience, which forces you to look within yourself. And to answer a call of nature, it's only a short walk, illuminated by the bright moonlight or a string of solar-powered twinkling fairy lights, to the nearby compost toilet. This bothy feels like it's good for your soul.

SWEENEY'S BOTHY

With its stunningly remote Hebridean location, this simple little bothy draws you to it naturally. A unique place of shelter and warmth, it inspires and facilitates creative work and expression. Its form is equally beautiful in both its material choices and its eco credentials, making it difficult not to want to be there.

OFF-GRID ARTIST'S RESIDENCE

For this innovative space on the Isle of Eigg, the "emerald of the Inner Hebrides," The Bothy Project's architect Iain Macleod teamed up with the artist Alec Finlay to create a dedicated off-grid artist's residence for Creative Scotland's Year of Natural Scotland 2013.

THE STRUCTURE

This zero-carbon dwelling was purpose-built for artists, writers, musicians, and the wider public to engage with the Scottish wilderness. Standing in a remote location overlooking the sea, it's an iconic hub for creative activity, which transmits information and inspiration on Scottish contemporary art, culture and ecology via a multimedia website.

INSPIRATION AND NARRATIVE

For his design, Alec Finlay was inspired by the legend of the cursed seventh-century Gaelic poet-king Sweeney, who fled into war-torn exile in the wilderness and survived for a decade on a diet of plants, berries and acorns. His poetry echoes the austere beauty of the remote glen where he lived naked and communed with animals and nature. The myth of Sweeney, the visionary hermit who rejected "feather beds and painted rooms" and chose instead to sleep in a thorn bush, still resonates with us today. This bothy belongs to a new contemporary movement, which Finlay identifies as "hutopian," whereby artists seek to create huts, cabins and viewing platforms as ecological, technological, architectural and social models in the wild and remote Scottish landscape. The simple modern design and renewable energy systems are in harmony with the green ethos of this beautiful island.

Using only natural building materials and representing the best of "hutopia" hut and cabin design, Sweeney's Bothy embodies sound architectural, ecological and technological principles. It stands beautifully proud in its lansdscape.

A POETIC PLAN

As Finlay puts it, in executing the plan there was a "constant interplay between poetic thought and hammer and nails" – this was a truly creative project. The starting point for the design and its central theme was the thorn, the emblem of Sweeney's years living in the wilderness. This would inform every aspect of the eco-cabin's structure and appearance, and the thorn became the formal pilotis-style support of the structure,

MATERIALS AND BUILD

The Bothy Project is committed to using sustainable, recycled materials and natural building techniques whenever possible, and Sweeney's Bothy is no exception. Natural building materials were chosen both inside and out to meld seamlessly into the windswept crofting and maritime landscape. Horizontal wooden planks provide the outer cladding and the surrounding deck, and the internal walls and floor are also constructed from wood. Even the little library snug has a wooden interior and seat. The sloping roof is made from corrugated metal with a rainwater harvesting system, and a layer of sheep's wool provides the insulation.

It took Bobby Niven of the Eigg project a whole winter to build, with the assistance of local residents, friends and family. This little building is suffused with a true community spirit, all part of a collaborative effort to establish art, crafts, music and media as a way of sustaining the local economy.

STYLE NOTES

This space, although almost spartan in its extreme simplicity, feels cozy and comfortable. The interior is welcoming and inviting with a fire burning brightly in the warm rustic hearth. The bothy has everything you need: space below to stretch out and live in, with a stove, a desk and an armchair, and a sleeping area above. A thorn-shaped wooden structure, echoing the thorn thicket in which Sweeney slept, supports a raised platform and bed, lifted up high like a bird's nest in the branches of a tree.

Although the thorns are symbolic of Sweeney's aloneness, they serve to inspire and challenge us to share this space creatively and heal our sense of isolation from the natural world. This is all about getting back to nature and the most fundamental pleasures in life: there's even a hot outdoor shower with a view. You can use it on a sunny summer's day, in a rainstorm or by starlight. And the floor-to-ceiling picture windows have amazing views, looking out across the sea to the Isle of Rum, and connecting you intimately with the external world.

Artists in residence and paying guests live off-grid when they visit this bothy. Indeed, the Isle of Eigg is not connected to the British national electricity grid, and power on the island is generated from renewable sources. The bothy generates its own electricity with two photovoltaic panels. Inside there's a wood-burning stove with an oven, and a well-equipped kitchen with a single gas ring but no refrigerator – a cooler and ice blocks are provided instead. When the sun's shining the hot water is provided by solar panels, but on cloudy days the boiler in the wood-burning stove kicks into action and takes over. And the refreshing pure-tasting water comes from a neighboring spring.

Careful attention has been paid to every detail to ensure that the bothy fulfills its eco-friendly credentials. There's a composting toilet; the furniture is recycled; there are organic fair-trade cotton bedding and towels; and even the duvet and mattress topper are made from organic wool. The artworks on display have been left behind by some of the artists who have lived and worked here, making the space seem more personal.

This simple cabin promotes a feeling of warmth and shelter, and rather than just being somewhere to escape from the elements, this is an outward-looking place to work. From the bench seats at the simple trestle desk/table in front of the large vertically paned plate glass window, the stunning aspect is over the rough, natural Hebridean landscape and the sea. It must be hard to stop yourself from starting to draw what so strongly holds your eye.

And at night, or when the weather roughens, the linen curtains cover the windows and create a more inward-looking space. Placing yourself in relatively social isolation and an often inclement environment can help to focus your mind, and doing so without too much roughing is certainly very appealing for many of us.

WAXED COTTON A-FRAME

Product designers Tom Gottelier and Bobby Peterson met at London's Royal College of Art and share a passion for working in a collaborative fashion. Over time their partnership developed to form the design studio Featuring-Featuring. Both of them particularly value working together with other designers, and in this case they have collaborated with the textile experimenter and designer Avanti Agarwal to create a simple wooden A-frame tent with a waxed, pigmented cotton covering.

THE PROJECT

Each year, the design group contributes a portion of its profits towards "Designers on Holiday," an annual design adventure on the Swedish island of Gotland. It runs over a three-week period and its purpose is to explore a variety of new ways for designers of different nationalities and disciplines to reintroduce themselves to the natural and creative side of design. Based at a campsite, the designers, known as "Holiday-Makers," are encouraged to collaborate, share and teach one another the tricks of their trades. At the end of the event it is opened to the public.

The builds can be varied, and as well as 18 tents there's a symbiotic hot tub, a luxury outdoor shower, a wood-fired bread oven, a one-man sauna, a terra-cotta kiln, a viewing platform, a waxed cotton sailing boat, an herbal distillery, a sound installation and a woodland cinema, together with a camp flag, a loom, soap fashioned from the local flora, paint pigments made from the land, many a wonderful dinner, a few ceramic plates and countless hand-carved spoons. A truly artistic experience.

STRUCTURE AND COLLABORATION

The 18 standard-issue white canvas tents are designed by the boys at Featuring-Featuring and supplied ready to build according to the plans. There's one for each Holiday–Maker designer. With a tent already assembled to act as a sample, each designer is encouraged to use it as a visual and practical starting reference point and to use their specific and individual skills, be they woodwork or sewing the canvas, to contribute to the collaborative effort to get all the tents built before nightfall. Once the basic structures have been built they are ready to be customized and modified by each designer as they wish, adding details such as legs, ladders, bedside tables and lamps.

In the spirit of this design collaboration, Tom and Bobby worked with the crafts-based designer and synesthete Avanti Agarwal. Inspired by the English tradition of waxing cotton to produce a waterproof material, she experimented with textiles and studied how Indian culture celebrates color and uses pigments in an intuitive and natural way. She explains that Tom saw her work and was "excited to push the experimentation on cotton. Together we create a process to melt the powdered, waxy pigment

Deceptively simple at first sight, this waxed A-frame tent isn't quite what it seems. It's shaped like a funnel 10 ft (3 m) high at the opening and reduces to 6 ft 6 in (2 m) at the back wall, so the views from inside the shelter are amplified. The covering cotton tent fabric is treated with powdered paraffin wax and pigment.

in order to produce colorful patterns whilst simultaneously waxing the clothing." The careful, hand-crafted technique of waxing the pattern onto the fabric was contrasted with simple mass-producible clothing designs, inventing an exciting new aesthetic for traditionally functional rain gear

An earlier collaborative project of theirs was to produce a clothing collection of waxed cotton, and from this sprung the irresistible idea of creating a scaled-up pigmented tent. Apart from the 18 regular tents, which can be assembled in a fraction of the time (albeit each one is customized), this "master tent" is a much larger structure, made with blue waxed cotton covering and taking two weeks to build.

"When we designed this we wanted it to be the focal point of the camp – something that really showed the collaboration between Featuring-Featuring and Avanti. We went for the traditional A-frame structure with a twist. The tent is 10 ft (3 m) high at the front and 6 ft 6 in (2 m) at the back, which makes it big enough for a fully grown adult to walk around inside – something we felt essential. The reasoning behind the difference in height from front to back was to create a funnel of sorts. When you sit up in bed and look out through the front of the tent the landscape is wonderfully framed, but working in reverse, from the large front opening to the smaller back one, it acts as a sound cone, funneling the noises of the surrounding landscape."

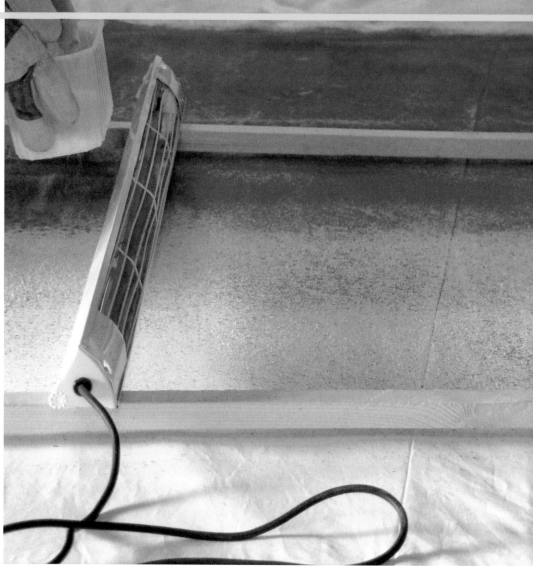

CONSTRUCTION AND FABRIC TECHNIQUE

For these intrepid product designers, creating the sturdy wooden framework was relatively simple. They used good-quality Swedish pine that could deal with the stresses of such a large tent in a strong wind. They started by sketching out the basic design on paper before making a CAD model to ensure they got the angles correct. "We worked by first constructing the platform around the rocky land it sits on – building it essentially into the landscape. Stilts connect the platform to the rock, either on smooth surfaces or plunging down the cracks."

Tom and Bobby decided that the tent should have a luxurious quality rather than be made purely of canvas, and they achieved this by building the back wall of the tent as a wooden piece with concealed cupboards. "We wanted a wall at the back that you could lean against in the morning to take in the view. But it also had to be capable of holding things rather than be just a wall – somewhere you could store your clothes, extra blankets and linens during your stay. The reason why the doors are hidden is quite nice. When it's time to dismantle the tent for winter you can open the cupboard doors and remove the bottom shelf to reveal a watertight hidden compartment

"we wanted a wall at the back that you could lean against in the morning to take in the view. But it also had to be capable of holding things rather than be just a wall – somewhere you could store your clothes, extra blankets and linens . . ."

that allows you to pack everything away neatly. We especially liked the idea that when everything is packed up with the canvas hidden away and the doors shut, the remaining structure would stay solid and totem-like in the landscape, waiting for next year's camp."

However, scaling up the fabric technique was more challenging because waxing the cotton on this larger scale required the construction of a more elaborate jig that could hold a heater from a chicken hatchery to melt the wax. The waxed cotton tent took exactly two weeks to make from the initial design to the finished item, including five days for waxing the cotton and sewing the fabric.

As Avanti recounts: "We wanted to stay as true to the process of waxed cotton as possible, so we used white cotton and then a mixture of powdered paraffin wax and pigment to create a speckled gradient. For the tent, we stuck with a very primary blue, as we felt that it blended well with the Swedish countryside and would look best framed against the blue summer sky." They didn't stop at just one tent, though, and soon moved on to a waxed wooden sailing boat with a pigmented waxed cotton sail. What a talented team they are!

PETE'S CLIFFTOP RETREAT

Pete's life and home, at the end of a clifftop path, are spectacular and inspiring. The aspect from on high, over the coast, the sea and the vast horizon, is unhindered – just like his spirit. He is a principled man who is driven by art, nature and practicality, someone who has really lived life and whose work has a life force all its own. He is always keen to use existing materials rather than new ones, and when a local convent was being pulled down he salvaged what was on offer. A relatively unexciting, 1960s building, this was an unprepossessing cube with square windows, but in Pete's mind the materials still had some life left in them and could be put to good use rather than be discarded.

DESIGN

With no definitive plan and from little more than a rough sketch and a desire to use the materials he had at hand, Pete decided to create a tall structure with an upper level on his land. He also planned an open-roofed section so he could sleep outdoors under the vast starlit sky. Making the design up in his head as he went along was his preferred route, using the lengths and qualities of the timber available to dictate the form. Since he did not want the building to feel enclosed, the structure is all about the view from the front, looking outwards over the cliff edge to the sea and sky.

THE LOCATION

The site is literally on the cliff edge, and looking down you can still see the ruins of an old hotel that suffered numerous misfortunes. After being burnt down in the 1950s it was demolished, but later, during an extremely high tide and before the sea defenses were built, the cliff collapsed along with the remnants of the building. You really are living on the edge here, plainly aware of the force and beauty of nature.

WORKING BY EYE

The ground needed leveling to create the foundations, which meant not only removing clumps but also picking out the lumps of concrete left over from the previous structures on the site. Preferring to use the natural horizon as his spirit level, Pete knelt down on the ground and, leveling his eyeline with the horizon, he started the build from there. Using new 3 x 2 graded sustainable timber for the structure of the main framework and his eye as the level, Peter gradually brought the building to life. Although it has a relatively small footprint, Pete wanted it to feel spacious and thus the building ended up being twice the size he had imagined.

Standing on a wide deck area and splaying out from the ground as it rises up, this clifftop retreat is an unconventional shape. The side walls are designed to open up by means of a top hinge via a simple flint counterweighted pulley system, so on good days the walls are raised to create an open-sided pavilion. Made from fabricated metal wire, flint-filled cubes, similar to those used locally as sea defenses, function as the counterweight to lift the side walls. Pete wanted the building to have visual integrity whether the sides were open or closed and to look as good either way. When they are closed, you have no idea that the walls are even capable of opening. When open, they are supported by four wooden posts, each wound in rope discarded from locally used crab pots, set into the deck and the roof.

Upstairs the outward-splaying shape continues, widening as it gets taller and also expanding towards the east and the sunrise with an upper sleeping level, glazed to the front over the cliff edge. However, the laws of physics dictated that this unconventional shape needed bracing in order to create strength and stability. By cladding the framework with reclaimed timber from the convent and the sliding roof with corrugated steel, the building gradually took shape.

PETE'S PHILOSOPHY

Pete's mantra is a reflection on his refreshing approach to life: "It's interesting to solve problems." He isn't scared of going off-trail, of finding his way and following an unconventional path. Aesthetically and practically, he is a very talented man and his innate spirit and energy complement his natural abilities and skills. This amazing building, together with its close neighbor known as the "Cliffhanger," is a courageous, individual, intriguing and vernacular structure. Pete says that it doesn't pay to make things overcomplicated and there's no benefit in doing things in a simple manner. He believes that carrying out projects on an absolute shoestring brings new creativity. If you haven't the option of buying something off the shelf or hiring someone else to do the work for you, you have to find a solution, and within that philosophy there's sometimes a very unexpected and wonderful answer.

THE PIGEON HOUSE

With a design inspired by the shape of a pigeon's breast, this building is both a cabin and a sculpture, albeit one that is functional and somewhere you can stay. On a big estate in the heart of rural England it's the focal point in a centuries-old agricultural landscape on the site of a former ramshackle barn. The old barn materials have been reused to create this site-specific cabin – an extraordinary gem and a lasting witness to its creator Tom Newton's unique creative view of the world.

THE CREATORS

Tom, a talented artist and designer, and his wife Sophy, a historian, are the managers of the Cotesbach Estate, a multifaceted heritage site. The estate, which once spread across vast acres of prime grazing, is now smaller but still a thriving rural hub, and the couple are acutely aware of its agricultural past. Tom is a skilled builder and craftsman, and all his projects are innovative, embodying a sense of freedom.

SHAPE AND PURPOSE

The tumbledown barn stood in the corner of a field on the estate on the edge of woodland, which was home to game birds, and Tom had the idea of now constructing there a small building shaped like a pigeon's breast. The woods are full of pigeons and they fly out across the fields. The purpose of the building would be to function as a shelter for agricultural pursuits or an occasional escape – a cozy overnight bothy, where people could stay and even roast a fresh pigeon or two for dinner.

PART-TIME BUILD

The initial drawings began, like so many good projects do, on the back of an envelope – it's the way Tom likes to do things. For him, the form follows the idea, which is central to the evolution of the build. In this case, the ovoid shape was inspired directly by the shape of the bird's breast and the build itself took a free-form style, using just Tom's eye. Without making use of any measurements or levels, the construction work began. Pragmatically, challenges were overcome in much the same way as any others in the normal course of a day's work. It was a part-time build with the walls going up over a three-month period in the summer of 2009 with Tom working on the building for three hours a day for half of each week. The challenge of creating the roof shape was more drawn out, and for five years it remained a simple felted roof structure before Tom tackled the challenge of creating its permanent concrete covering.

This unique and creative build is inspired by the shape of a pigeon's breast. Built using locally sourced building materials, it has a simple but intriguing form. Its gray-finished curving concrete roof and rounded brick façade reflect the spirit and belief with which it has been created.

REUSING MATERIALS

Tom and Sophy's preference is to reuse as many existing materials as possible, and some of the bricks used in the construction were the remains of the former brick-built barn that had stood on the site. Additional bricks and cobbles came from the estate's stable yard, where a 10 ft (3 m) high wall between the top stables and the former kennels had fallen down. Around each of the windows and the door opening are rounded bricks from the end section of the collapsed wall. They were purposely rounded to prevent the jostling livestock on their way to the milking parlor and cowshed from bumping themselves on the angular brick corners. Tom cleaned the bricks as he went along, using every piece possible. With their characteristic strongly red tone, they are locally made and used for many of the homes and farm buildings in the surrounding villages.

For the construction timber, larch was utilized because of its durability. The roof form was a material challenge: although Tom had considered using the more traditional thatch or shingles, in the end concrete won out due to its ability not only to accommodate the distinctive curved form but also its capacity for an integral storm drain. The window openings have vertically sliding shutters to close them, while the window in the door is deliberately ovoid in shape to add even more character to this quirky build.

THE INTERIOR

This is a really interesting interior space – part practical shelter and part charming romantic escapist folly. The central feature is the free-standing wood-burning stove, which previously had been in service elsewhere on the estate. The floor is roughly cobbled and the windows are just unglazed simple openings. On the bed is a large, colorful woolen patchwork blanket, which tells its own special story. Sophy explains that "during the 1970s we used to spend all our holidays in Ireland in Creetown, Galloway, where my mother discovered a woolen mill. She snapped up a whole load of fabric scraps and "seconds" at some sale or other and sewed them all together into this gorgeous blanket, which my parents had on their bed for years, and it still keeps us warm today."

Other items come from elsewhere in the main house, and many of them have their own family story, too, including the old Fortnum & Mason attractive wicker hamper basket, an earthenware mustard jar, and a Christmas cookie tin that Sophy's grandfather gave them in 1992, along with his special bone-handled, steel-bladed knife from Paris and a three-tined fork. Even the bread knife is 25 years old.

"the form follows the idea, which is central to the evolution of the build. In this case, the ovoid shape was inspired directly by the shape of the bird's breast and the build itself took a free-form style . . ."

The inside of the Pigeon House is a simple shelter, a rustic den. The unglazed window openings have vertical sliding shutters. The bricks edging the windows are curved, reflecting the light entering the building in a soft and luminous way. The blankets have been in Sophy's family for years and she has even made a patchwork bed cover from them. These small gestures of warmth and comfort lift the space, creating a rustic hideaway like no other.

STYLE NOTES

Referencing nature in its form, its use of materials and its function, this is a unique elemental cabin. It also has character, taking its shape from a bird rather than the traditional oblong form with an apex roof. The interior has a painterly quality – it's rough and ready with rustic windows that are simple openings and an uneven cobbled floor. The stove radiates warmth and makes it feel cozy and homely. Sophy has furnished the cabin with old family pieces, each with worn tones and warm textures.

This cabin feels remote and historical, despite the fact that it's relatively newly built, but just how many pigeon-shaped buildings do you come across? In this context the building looks entirely at home – unsurprisingly so, because, apart from its unusual form, each of the materials came from less than a few hundred yards away. Visually arresting, the exterior form is extraordinary but it still manages to be convincing. Here, tucked into the intersection of the fields and woods, it feels right at home.

CARRAIG FIREPLACE

Looking out over the Canadian Rocky Mountains and Ghost Lake in the foothills of southern Alberta is Carraig Ridge. This abstract yet witty outdoor fireplace, which was created as the first of three unusual modern landscape follies, sits on the banks of Lake Anna. The surrounding 650 acres (263 ha) are being used to build country homes.

INSPIRED BY A WOOD STACK

Inspired by the form of a stack of wood and a development on the idea of the conventional fire pit around which people always love to gather, this modern take creates a habitable space, a loose and open enclosure around the hearth. Not fully protected and still engaged with the great outdoors and the incredible landscape, it acts as a focal point and social space where the simple and humble elements of an open outdoor fire are maintained with a modicum of human shelter.

THE BUILD

Designed over a four-week period with the focus on using materials that would be readily available, it was built using straightforward construction methods. In order to minimize the construction time on-site and to limit any damage to the natural wetland ecosystem, the build took two months in a controlled environment, with each timber section cut to size, aligned and fastened together as a "test fit" in the design shop of XYC Design + Development in Alberta. From there the piece was disassembled into sections, transported to the site and reassembled within a week.

MATERIALS

The two principal materials are untreated 4 x 6 fir timber, which weathers attractively over time, and polished stainless steel caps that reflect the Rocky Mountain foothill landscape in their finish. The floor and fire pit itself are made of recycled materials. The timber, locally sourced, was cut into 3 ft (0.9 m) and 5 ft (1.5 m) lengths and placed in six different positions in an interpretation of a stack of firewood. The surface is thick and substantial, giving a sense of shelter, while being open and filtering the outdoor views. A single large, unglazed picture window completes the build.

DESIGN PHILOSPHY

Acutely aware of our generation's reliance upon digital methodologies and clinically dictated solutions, lead architect Bryan Young of the design studio Young Projects in New York City prefers the conscious introduction of the "analog." Here he has combined it with some willful nuances and anomalies, together with other natural forces that generate differences and a richly layered end result.

So even in what is essentially a contemporary "techie" approach to the design of this highly unusual fireplace, the human touch and thought processes always hover near the surface, there to be seen. The end result is, in effect, a remarkably successful working partnership between digital design and craft, which is not only open to a range of influences and possibilities but, beyond that, also informs the material choices. It's all part of Bryan Young's design philosophy and aesthetic.

According to the architect, "the piling method creates a thick yet porous exterior, offering a sense of shelter while providing filtered views to the exterior. A single open picture window reconnects an occupant with the foreground of Lake Anna and the surrounding hills."

STYLE NOTES

This is a fresh and inspiring take on creating a small enclosure, a witty expression grounded in good principles. On completion, this solution looks deceptively simple, but not when you're starting with a blank piece of paper. The stack of firewood, assembled in the manner of constructing a real fire and crisscrossing the kindling to get it started, is an inspired reference. The neat wood stacks go beyond their fundamental purpose and are equally inspiring pieces of temporary sculpture.

We all love an open fire with its warm glow and the light from the flickering flames. The reflections of the landscape in the two materials used, as well as the light-toned wood and the stainless steel finishings, echo this to create an atmosphere and sense of being comfortably enclosed. And, of course, the human factor plays large: it's a gathering point. There's the usual domestic feature of a large picture window, but here you're not totally inside or outside – all around you is this just incredible natural landscape. Bryan Young and his team have brought together some basic elements and found the appropriate inspiration points to achieve something clever and beautiful with a few simple pieces.

CARRAIG FIREPLACE

HOLIDAYS

When you want to take a break and just chill, what could be more relaxing than escaping to a cool cabin, cottage or summerhouse far away from modern urban living? These unique builds are in areas of outstanding natural beauty, often not only off the beaten track but off-grid, too, where you can reconnect with nature and recharge your batteries before returning to the familiar routines of everyday life. They are the vision of some enterprising people who are blessed with entrepreneurial drive as well as a creative eye.

A seaside 1950s-style "shack" on the Isle of Wight summons up nostalgic memories of idyllic childhood holidays from years ago with its sensitive vintage feel. Further north, on a wooded hillside overlooking Lake Windermere in the visually stunning Lake District, another shack has been transformed into a three-story eco-dwelling. It may have a small footprint, but the clever design and light interior make it feel like a large space; it's a little gem.

Scandinavian style, art and culture are very much in vogue, and the fishing cabin belonging to the cinematographer Bengan Widell on the island of Gotland is a simple yet stylish example of this phenomenon. Inside he has combined the perfect mix of stripped Swedish pine and North African artifacts. Surprisingly, this unusual approach is a marriage made in heaven. Meanwhile, the Stockholm-based designer Anna-Karin Nyfjäll has used her creativity and design skills to transform her family's tumbledown seaside cabin into a comfortable summerhouse. It's simple, beautiful yet unpretentious – nautical but not drab. This simplicity is reflected in another Swedish summerhouse, designed by the founder of Rumbler furniture. Inspired by traditional local crafts and using the best-quality materials, he has created something timeless yet contemporary. All these spaces are considered, neat, uncluttered and minimalist in their approach and appeal.

And, lastly, we move on from the cool color palette of northern Europe to the warmer climate and vivid hues of the south, where in Portugal a businessman has created two imaginative luxury holiday venues. These award-winning eco-friendly cabanas echo the simplicity of their Swedish cousins and blend seamlessly into the natural landscape, helping visitors to disconnect with the material world and embrace a gentler way of living.

THE SHACK

On the Isle of Wight, off the south coast of England, Helen and Frazer have created a collection of unique places to stay – from vintage Airstreams, 1950s scout huts and a former evangelical tin tabernacle to this holiday "shack." This visionary couple are blessed with a creative eye, as well as drive and courage, and their properties not only have enormous integrity and authenticity but also have been beautifully restored and styled in keeping with the feeling and look of the original function and life of each space. This simple seaside wooden cabin has a masterful twist in the story, and even though it was a modern build, all its vintage charm and character have been skillfully created.

HIDDEN CHARMS

Helen and Frazer had successful careers in photography and styling in London when they did what many of us dream of but don't always achieve. They moved lock, stock and barrel out of the city to create a new life and business for themselves, running "vintage vacations." Starting with just one beautiful Airstream trailer, their business has grown steadily without losing any of its original charm and professionalism.

THE ACQUISITION

Not long after selling their London house, this enterprising couple spotted "The Shack" among the multitude of bungalows and holiday flats in a real estate agent's window. It was a small, modern and not particularly attractive holiday chalet of wooden construction, and although it didn't have the right credentials for the "vintage" look they were seeking, the location was great and they recognized its potential for the requisite charm and good looks it needed to succeed as a holiday rental. Their very first purchase, it tempted their palette for future outlays and it was soon followed by an old scout hall and a mission hut.

The charms of The Shack were not plain to see initially, since it stood among a selection of ramshackle sheds, old railway carriages and some more recently built cabins. However, the location was special – hidden, serene, beautiful and off the beaten track – and it clinched the deal.

THE PROJECT

Newly purchased and christened "The Shack," this building was a nasty orange pine chalet. It lacked vintage charm and potential buyers would have been put off by its appearance. However, its newness meant that it was solidly constructed, it wasn't damp and it didn't leak. Helen and Frazer realized, in a way familiar to people who work in the film industry, that they needed to "age it down" to remove the newness of the building and also to add a dose of charm and nostalgia for a bygone age. Frazer is reasonably competent at DIY and does a lot of the work himself, along with some help from the professionals, while Helen, as an experienced stylist, "art directs" and is practically skilled and good with her hands.

"they found inspiration in the older cabins and the traditional color schemes of period seaside homes . . ."

CHALLENGES

Adding charm to an otherwise charmless new structure was an interesting challenge for the couple, who "had to put the grit back into the place." They had an image in their heads of what an archetypal period seaside retreat should look like and yet they were faced with a very new and boring space. Undeterred, they took up the challenge.

To add texture and character, Helen and Frazer installed tongue-and-groove paneling on the walls. Another – and more obvious – contribution towards the process of making the chalet more beautiful and less modern looking was simply to paint it. Looking at the other properties on the same site, they found inspiration in the older cabins clustered around them, and in the traditional color schemes and combinations that are unique and particular to period seaside holiday homes. By painting "The Shack" and building a small shingle-clad extension, they transported it right into their "vintage" purview.

What can be seen as an asset and a key to a building's "specialness" can also present some issues and complications. "The Shack" was certainly in a beautiful location and "tucked away," but that also meant it was off the main road or, indeed, any road. Located down a bumpy old farm track, it was off-grid without main utilities apart from running water. Helen and Frazer added a solar power source for modern essentials: running the lighting, powering a small radio and, of course, charging a mobile phone. Water is heated, the refrigerator kept cool and the stove fueled by propane bought in canisters. General heating is provided by the wood-burning stove, while the lavatory is a composting toilet.

The couple were cautious, too, and knowing that this was going to be an important part of their holiday rental property business they did their due diligence and checked that the terms of the lease allowed such a use before going ahead with the initial purchase.

Creating a restful and comfortable atmosphere is something most of us long for. Using her stylist's eye, Helen has done far more than building something good to look at. Besides the beautiful vignettes is a home away from home, a modern take on the classic English seaside holiday of the past.

THE INTERIOR

An occupational hazard for most stylists, apart from those with an iron will, is that along the way you start to acquire and keep the things you really like. They might be unusual objects that were exceptionally hard to source or ones that are particularly used, worn and beautiful, or things that are so deliciously on the borders of bad taste that they are actually incredibly cool and destined to become the next fashionable "must have" trend. This helps to explain why good stylists are good stylists, in a nutshell.

Helen fits into this category, and her collection boxes of "stuff" from her styling days included a pair of 1960s wooden-framed armchairs, which had a touch of utility and just about fit into the space. Also in her "stash" was a pair of old worn Union Jack flags, made from natural fibers with the different colored sections stitched together. The Isle of Wight, too, is a great source of vintage interior items and nautical bric-a-brac. Helen has a genuine love for these things, a sharp eye and a good instinct, as well as a garage full to the brim with vintage kitchen units. The local stores do a good job of replenishing her stylist's stock cupboard with vintage finds. The kitchen, in particular, needed a good dose of vintage charm and character, and into that space went an old dresser, along with some pink Formica for a period touch. A vintage caravan stove was sourced and it was all pulled together with some custom-made cabinetry.

**"it feels authentic, it's beautiful and it reminds us of our childhood holidays, a favorite aunt's seaside home.
It's a place where any of us would be happy to hang out, spend some time, and just be . . ."**

STYLE NOTES

To create a space like this, which is convincing yet started as a charmless new build, is inspiring and commendable. However, you need to have the vision straight off, and to retain it through a carefully thought-out plan of renovation, "aging down" and adding character. This process has to start with the building itself – its structure, the materials and textures, and the color scheme. It's easy to think of "vintage" as textiles and small dressings, but color choice and patina are the bedrock on which it all has to sit.

And that all this came about from Helen and Frazer looking at an unprepossessing modern building in a real estate agent's window and seeing its potential for creating an authentically styled vintage seaside cabin is amazing. The steps they took and the inspiration they found by looking around them are valuable lessons for us all. They kept their vision throughout, and chose a color scheme of off-white, muted blue and pale gray that was just right for the seaside location and a small cabin-like building. They also used brighter highlights of color: blue externally and flashes of vivid pink on the kitchen worktops to echo the 1950s and '60s that the cabin visually references. They add a realness, too, a sense of the genuine, the human touch. In the bedroom, Helen's collection of bamboo-edged mirrors is put to good use, hung together all on one wall, reflecting the sea and adding a touch of space and lightness.

The result of this extraordinary project could have been a pastiche, something lovely but impractical and unconvincing from a glossy magazine, but it isn't. Instead, it feels authentic, it's beautiful and it reminds us of our childhood holidays, a favorite aunt's seaside home. It's a place where any of us would be happy to hang out, spend some time, and just be. Helen sums it up very well: "As with all our holiday lets, it was a bit of a leap of faith to buy it. We weren't sure if other people would like it or find the area as magical as we did. But we needn't have worried – The Shack has many regular guests and three volumes of heartwarming visitors' book comments . . . we are genuinely moved by some of them – poems and all!"

BENGAN'S COTTAGE

When the cinematographer Bengan Widell isn't working on films and traveling around the world, he can be found on the Swedish island of Gotland, indulging his passion for renovating old rural buildings.

THE STRUCTURE

This rustic little wooden house by the sea was once a spartan fisherman's hut, used only for storing nets and fishing rods, lines and equipment. When Bengan came across it, it was very run down, derelict and overgrown with trees and bushes. One of its most appealing features is its remote location, only 33 ft (10 m) away from the sea but more than 0.6 miles (1 km) from the nearest house, making it a very quiet and peaceful place – a tranquil retreat for Bengan after all his globetrotting.

A SPEEDY RENOVATION

When Bengan's not away on location, he's happiest living beside the sea. Discovering the fishing shack changed his life and it only took him just over a month to renovate the cottage and clear the land around it. Nature had completely taken over and you could hardly see the shed, which was hidden by branches, foliage, creepers and undergrowth.

OFF-GRID LIFESTYLE

Bengan's plan was to renovate and refurbish the building and transform it into a cozy cottage where he could stay all year-round. He wanted to retain the essential character of the 100-year-old structure, so as much as possible he used only recycled traditional materials, all purchased locally. The shack was off-grid and he didn't attempt to install electricity or a modern heating and lighting system, preferring to stick with kerosene lamps, candles and a wood-burning stove.

MATERIALS AND BUILD

The shack was in a poor state when Bengan started work, and the roof, some wall panels, ceilings, windows and floors all needed replacing. He found some of the wood as well as recycled windows in a local secondhand shop – the rest of the wooden panels and floorboards came from a nearby farmer with his own sawmill. Nothing was wasted and even the imposing bed was made from the trees he cut down when he cleared the space around the house. To weatherproof the cottage, so it could withstand the harsh Scandinavian winters and the wind-driven salty spray from the sea, he treated the wooden exterior with a powerful mixture of tar, turpentine and linseed oil.

STYLE NOTES

Inside this little wooden gem of a house, everything is ordered and calm. It's a rustic space with an unusual mix of stripped Swedish pine and vintage Moroccan artifacts, lamps and rugs. Incredibly, the North African accents don't seem out of place and they complement the muted, natural colors and textures of the wood. Everything has been reduced to the basic necessities of everyday living. There's a traditional wood-burning stove to heat the space and for cooking, a gas fridge, a rustic wooden table and chairs, and some baskets for carrying and storing logs. The Moroccan kerosene lamps, with their colored glass, emit a comforting soft glow when the sun goes down.

One of the pleasures of living here for Bengan is lying in bed and just feasting on the amazing view from the window. "You can see the ocean a few meters away. There are beautiful sunrises in the morning, moonbeams rippling on the water at night, and sometimes spectacular thunderstorms that suddenly appear over the bay after the summer heat."

Outside on the wooden porch there's a hammock, a rectangular wooden trestle table and some fold-up camping chairs where you can sit and watch the sunset. During the summer Bengan cooks outside for his daughters and friends on a little propane stove and they eat under a clear, unpolluted sky peppered with millions of stars. For him, this simple rural retreat is the perfect antidote to his busy working life in the media – a place where he can really chill out and relax.

"there are beautiful sunrises in the morning, moonbeams rippling on the water at night, and sometimes spectacular thunderstorms that suddenly appear . . ."

STYLE SUMMARY

Style-wise it's really interesting to observe the mixing of decorative elements from differing cultures: the Nordic stove, the colorful Moroccan lamps, the striped rugs, the enamel kitchenware – a surprising and unusual mix but, together, they look convincing and work successfully as a whole. There are three reasons why this works. Each of the elements is authentic, a genuine artifact from a particular country or of that style rather than a rehash of a vintage style. Secondly, each item reflects the touch of the human hand – the lanterns look hand-beaten, the rugs simply woven on a loom, and the stone on which the fire sits was found by someone, and is rich in texture and handcrafted. And, lastly, there is just about the right amount, sitting comfortably in the midground between a simple sparse interior and a cluttered one. There are enough interesting items and details to engage you as your eye passes slowly and enjoyably around the space.

THE LOVE SHACK

Karen and Adam Guthrie are a very creative couple with a passion for art and collecting beautiful objects, especially ceramics, pottery and textiles. Adam is the curator and director of Grizedale Arts, a contemporary arts residency in the Lake District, while Karen is not only an artist and filmmaker but also one of the designers of an innovative community garden regeneration project near Olympic Park in London.

THE STRUCTURE

The Love Shack, which acquired its affectionate name from the diminutive size of the original cabin, is a unique three-story dwelling with impressive eco credentials. Designed by the acclaimed Sutherland Hussey Architects in Edinburgh, it's a spacious timber-clad building that is surprisingly modern and innovative. It has an open-plan living space with a modern kitchen and a dining area with French doors opening out onto an elevated wooden deck. There's a double bedroom on the semi-mezzanine floor above, a bathroom with woodland views and a detached garden studio. This well-designed compact space is the perfect size for a couple.

INSPIRATION AND INFLUENCES

Karen and Adam wanted to find somewhere to live for a few months while their home was being renovated, and they fell in love with a secluded old log cabin set into the hillside in a wooded location overlooking Lake Windermere. They were hooked by the stunning scenery and idyllic views and decided to transform the decaying tiny cabin into a luxurious retreat. In spite of the basic 1960s interior and rather austere exterior, the cabin had character and these two idealists saw the potential to create a sustainable modern home away from home. And finding a sympathetic architect was easy; Sutherland Hussey have designed many iconic contemporary buildings in rural settings and, what's more, Charlie Sutherland is Adam's brother.

They wanted to create a really unique and beautiful building, which was environmentally sensitive and comfortable. They were inspired by a wide range of influences, ranging from Japanese traditional architecture to films such as *The Ice Storm*. Perhaps their biggest motivation was the desire to encourage people with an interest in self-building to break the mold and embrace contemporary architectural styles, designs and construction techniques in traditional rural settings.

The style of the building and the Love Shack's location in a national park were both key factors in choosing an architectural style and materials that were delicate, sympathetic and well thought out.

CHALLENGES

When they embarked on this labor of love, Karen and Adam had no idea that it would be such a lengthy, costly and tortuous process to obtain the necessary planning permission. The Lake District is designated a national park, which creates additional complications, and the planning alone included a public hearing that is normally reserved for major projects such as proposed new motorways and airports and took five years before the building project began. On-site construction was ongoing for nearly two more years.

One of the biggest problems they encountered on this build was the stipulation by the planners that no heavy machinery would be allowed onto the site, so everything had to be physically carried there by people. This was challenging because not many construction workers were willing to do this heavy-lifting work. Even digging a hole for a septic tank had to be done in the time-honored way with a spade.

To establish its green credentials and prevent impacting the surrounding tree roots, which were protected by a Tree Preservation Order, the usual building methods of laying the foundations with bricks and mortar were not permissible. Instead, the structure was built on 4 in (100 mm) diameter steel rods – "mini piles" – driven into the ground by hand. And the physical layout of the site, which was exceptionally steep and so difficult to work on, was yet another challenge, especially in the absence of heavy machinery.

MATERIALS AND BUILD

Local materials were utilized wherever possible for the build, thereby reducing the carbon footprint. Mainly reclaimed local cedar was used for the interior while the sawmill on the neighboring Graythwaite Estate supplied the exterior timber from trees in the forest behind the house. A system of quickly assembled structural insulated panels (SIPs) with external larch cladding keeps the house warm and snug in winter. Although larch is a soft wood, it is extremely weatherproof and rot-resistant, being full of resin, and because the grade is very consistent the color and texture are uniform throughout. What's more, it doesn't require any treatment and it should last for 20 years before it needs replacing.

Most of the on-site heavy construction work, as well as the interior carpentry (with the exception of the kitchen cabinets), was carried out by local builders and skilled craftsmen. However, as the months went by, deadlines passed and the financial crisis took hold, Karen and Adam lost some of their builders and they ended up having to finish off some of the work themselves, including the external cladding, which they secured with a nail gun.

Overall, there was a lot of troubleshooting on this project. The well-insulated house is heated by a wood-burning stove, sitting flush to the living room wall, but because the walls are wooden it proved difficult to find skilled tradespeople who were willing to do the fireproofing, so Karen ended up reading the building regulations and doing it herself. The chrome flue has become an attractive external feature.

The flat roof is now home to an exotic green mixture of moss, grasses and ferns, helping to camouflage it within the surrounding foliage. The wonderful thing about this build is how little impact it's made on an area of outstanding natural beauty and how the materials used have blended seamlessly into the environment.

At the other end of the "rustic" spectrum from the original wood cabin, the Love Shack's interior captures the available light. Lined with light-toned wood and with the sunlight reflecting off the white and pale gray painted surfaces, the interior architecture, furnishings and finishes combine to redefine modern rustic.

STYLE NOTES

The color palette is modern, natural and visually gentle. Outside, the cladding has aged and faded to a delicate silvery gray – it's not crisp, abrasive or sterile but looks like it's always been like that. Light filters through the trees into the house, making it softer and greener in summer, cooler in winter. The clever use of wood makes it feel warm and cozy. The same oak parquet flooring has been used throughout, and in the "man cave" garden room recycled wood scraps have been assembled in a jigsaw block style. This well-seasoned wood with its lovely white acrylic finish was purchased at a local undertaker's sale – the wood was originally intended for making coffins.

Although this space has a footprint of only 592 sq ft (55 sq m), the intelligent design makes it feel much larger. It's the details that count: the front door and entrance are huge, giving an impression of spaciousness. And the interior isn't cluttered or crammed with objects – everything has been chosen carefully and the overall feel is light and luxurious. Most of the Love Shack is furnished and decorated with Japanese simplicity, including the deep square bath and tactile cork wallpaper in the bathroom, but the garden room is more ornate with an Ercol midcentury daybed, a gilded ormolu chair and an old wooden desk. The record player and vinyl LPs pay testament to a long-gone musical age. This couple loves mixing the old with the new. Their creative background has influenced their style, and as a filmmaker Karen wanted to create a beautiful "set" for living. This restorative space encompasses many modern luxuries and high-tech gadgets – a flat-screen TV, a DVD player and library, an iPod dock and wireless broadband, a halogen cooktop and combination oven/microwave – but it's still close to the natural world. And it's romantic – there's even a Juliet balcony outside the bedroom overlooking the deck. For Karen and Adam it's a joy, and you can enjoy it, too, as this enterprising couple rent it out when they're not using it.

"the Love Shack gives us so much pleasure to own and look at . . . it's a little gem, like a Fabergé egg . . ."

ANNA-KARIN'S SUMMERHOUSE

Swedish-based Anna-Karin Nyfjäll has a love of design that crosses over several areas, from interior design to floristry. For her, good design is at the heart of everything and this finds expression both in her life and work. The owner of the acclaimed Stockholm store In the Mood, she puts her heart and soul into finding the right items not only for the shop but also for her home. Rather than following a set "look," the creative mix, character and overall feeling are equally important to her.

THE HISTORY

This seaside cabin had been in Anna-Karin's family for many years – her mother-in-law was born in the house – and it was used as a retreat every summer. But although it was lovely and charmingly ramshackle, it was not perfect. It was too small and Anna's family was growing in the sense that her teenage children's lives were extending, too, so she decided to enlarge it, making it big enough to accommodate the whole family, plus her children's entourage of boyfriends and girlfriends. After throwing a midsummer party in the house, she realized that, with a bit of work, this could become more of a home. With the agreement and help of the whole family, and over a two-year period, they all set about carrying out the sensitive development from seaside cabin to summerhouse.

PRIORITIES

Although it stood in an incredible coastal location, the house was, in essence, basic and not in a habitable state – apart from the main structure, it was in "shell" form without proper floors, heating or fittings. The family's immediate priorities were to install a floor and heating but, without doubt, their biggest challenge was to make the absolute best of the available space. The essential requirement was that it needed to be able to accommodate a minimum of four people at any one time. In order to keep the spending budget manageable, Anna-Karin and her family took on the work themselves and did everything except the main window wall installation, for which they used specialist contractors.

MATERIALS

Anna-Karin liked the soul of this house – its age and traditional character – so her preference for the renovation was to use only materials that matched the age of the house and had the same worn, comfortable feel. However, at the other end of the spectrum is reality. Aesthetics always need to be balanced with practicality, and the house needed to be livable, workable and easy to take care of and maintain. By keeping all the original features and using wood for almost everything else, the family reinvented the house in a more livable version of its former self.

Cladding the walls and underside of the open eave space with horizontal wood paneling, and painting all the surfaces white other than the natural gray wood floor, gives a cohesive light space to the tiny interior with its multifunctional spaces. A ladder to climb up to the mezzanine bedroom is fixed vertically to the wall so not to lose any floor space.

The totally glass end wall opening onto the deck, and Anna-Karin's style of using furniture that could be used in an inside space, such as the wooden daybeds rather than outdoor loungers, adds to the sense of a larger living area and indoor-outdoor living. The furniture adds a sense of permanence.

DECORATION

The form of the building is a simple apex shape, which is open inside right up to the roof. A mezzanine bedroom is open to the main living space, and the interior is lined with rough horizontal cladding, simply painted white. Interestingly, Anna-Karin sees this more in terms of its qualities of brightness than tone: "We decided that we wanted bright colors on the walls, as the floor is gray. All the details are colorful." The small kitchen area is also open to the main space set against the mezzanine wall divide.

Stylistically, Anna-Karin looked to the locality, to the beachfront and the ocean, and used authentic and genuine pieces rather than a pastiche. She was especially attracted to items with natural worn textures. "I'm inspired by the ocean and I've bought a lot of things from flea markets and antique shops that are connected with the sea."

ATMOSPHERE

Inside the cabin the atmosphere is relaxed and comfortable, beautiful but not precious. The interior functions as a comfort, a counterpoint and a shelter, but it's outward- rather than inward-looking, focused on the light, the wooden deck and the beach outside. The large glazed wall and equally large deck exaggerate this, and lounging is actively encouraged whether you're inside or out. "The atmosphere is very light and bright. The sun shines almost every day, and the wind's always blowing, which is good for surfing."

STYLE NOTES

Anna-Karin's style is unpretentious but comfortable; it's relevant to its location and purpose and it's how she's gone about achieving this that is interesting. Her approach is simplicity itself: "My philosophy is that you should have a simple life when you're on vacation, not do too much and just enjoy the people around you." To achieve this, however, takes more than just having a simple interior and putting a few nautical collectibles together. She has chosen a formal layout of furniture together with rich and varied textures and used items that have a patina. Even the furniture is laid out with a symmetry: there's a similar chair on either side of the large glass door, the sofa is set casually but with a pair of mismatching cushions, and the round coffee table links everything in the space together.

The textures, too, are considered and thoughtful. There are hard surfaces of older unfinished wood, woven jute and wicker, gleaming glass and stainless steel. The shiny modern is set against the rough and rustic, and it works. The softer materials follow suit with natural sheepskins on the wicker chairs, and ethnic patterns on the bedspreads on the daybed/loungers outside and on the cushion covers inside.

Above all, it is nautical but not drab: the ship's lantern is genuine and life-worn, as well as the trunks. The sense of the journey is in there, too. It tells a tale, takes you with it and isn't just one-dimensional. The different elements and items – the textures, pieces and life itself – are all set out within the quiet formality, imperceptibly weaving the home comforts and the simple atmosphere together.

RUMBLER SUMMERHOUSE

This quintessentially Swedish summerhouse was created by furniture designer Lars Hofsjö, the founder of Rumbler and experimental platform Hofsjö, together with his colleague John Larsson for Lars' cousin, who lives in Los Angeles but returns to her homeland every summer for a family holiday. Lars is multitalented, and as well as being a successful industrial designer, he's a skilled carpenter and interior designer and did a lot of the construction work himself.

THE STRUCTURE

Although this summerhouse was actually built in the 1960s, it feels and looks much older. It's one of four red-painted houses built around a farmhouse in the countryside one hour's drive south of Stockholm.

INSPIRATION

Lars was inspired by traditional Swedish crafts and his own contemporary designs. He wanted to bring these together in a happy marriage in an unassuming house, adding his own distinctive ergonomic touches. It would not only be the result of his design philosophy and passion but also made and shaped by his own hands because he planned to work on it himself.

As he says: "I wanted to incorporate modern and minimal design with a nod to history and quality craftsmanship." Right from the beginning his plan was to use traditional hardwoods, classic hand-painted and stenciled wallpaper, and reclaimed building and architectural materials from junk shops, antique stores and flea markets. "Seeing the beauty in these materials is what inspired me to dabble with several modern concepts and incorporate them within the farmhouse." His inspiration came from handmade quality crafts and he took these and reinvented them in a minimalist style, making them more relevant to contemporary living.

PLANNING IT OUT

Lars' original idea was to use only high-end and reused materials and traditional "old-school" techniques for this project. It's quite a large structure and the renovation was very labor intensive, requiring him to work from September to June and stretching over a two-year period. During the first year, he worked there for two to three days per week, cutting back to a maximum of four days per month the following year.

The owners of the summerhouse, Viveca Paulin and Will Ferrell, gave Lars complete freedom to make all the renovation and design decisions. Everything was carefully planned from the early designs and demolition work right through to the color palette, furniture, decoration and objects.

Adding large windows and removing previous improvements where the materials were cheap or fake cleared the way for the interiors to be simple and uncluttered. Better-quality materials and interior furnishings helped to create a calming and comfortable space.

MATERIALS AND BUILD

The plan was to use the best-quality materials available – ones that would age gracefully and aesthetically with the passing of time. All the prerenovation cheap or fake materials in the house were taken out and replaced with solid hardwood: massive wooden planks for the floor and hand-chiseled planks for the ceilings. Silky smooth marble tiles and countertops and sandstone mounted sinks were installed, while hand-torn paper sheets with visible rough overlapping edges were used as wall coverings in some rooms. As an experienced designer and craftsman, Lars is familiar with construction work, and the skills needed for many tasks are not a problem for him. He's good at troubleshooting and coming up with practical solutions to any challenges that arise. "I always think that everything is possible – you just need to figure out how. And you need some really good tools as well."

The initial demolition and renovation work was heavy and dirty. Lars' plan was to tackle it gradually, stage by stage, rather than gut the whole building. He likes to adopt an orderly approach and clear away the trash from one area at a time to keep the workspace clean and uncluttered. The most challenging room was the "studio." Dark and gloomy, it had a low ceiling and plastic floor covering. Lars commissioned two big windows from a local carpenter to let in the light and took everything out, even the ceiling. Above it was an attractive roof made out of large pieces of wood and this opened up the space. The wooden planks from the original ceiling were recycled.

FURNITURE AND OBJECTS

Many of Lars' signature pieces are featured, including his distinctive rag rugs, which he transforms into extraordinary tables. His mother used to make beautiful rag rugs on a loom set up in her bedroom when he was a child, and he wanted to give their design a modern twist and, in so doing, to pay his respects to the craftswomen who have made these traditional floor coverings.

This exciting project really fired his imagination, and many of the objects he now sells evolved from the prototypes that were designed and made specially for Viveca and Will's house – his Nord storage and sitting solution is a case in point. Inspired by the pine plank floors in the summerhouse, it was designed with subtle variations in color, size and shape to add diversity to the overall scheme.

Other classic items of furniture include a silvery Tolix chair, over which is draped a luxurious, tactile fur throw, at the old metal writing table in the bedroom. Lars also added his own pieces to the space, including some Rumbler chairs, storage boxes and rag-rug tables. Interestingly, his own brand, Hofsjö, was inspired by the quality materials he worked with during the renovation of the house.

STYLE NOTES

Inside, this house looks very old and you could easily feel as though nothing has changed in over a century, but in reality many of the elements and pieces that appear to be timeless are actually very modern indeed. Simplicity is key to the success of the design and, consequently, the interior has a gentle, uncluttered feel. You get the impression that everything included has been chosen with exquisite care and consideration. The space feels warm and cozy with the wooden-paneled walls, ceilings and floors. The rag rugs add a welcome splash of color and a rough texture to the smooth, rather austere interior.

"I wanted to incorporate modern and minimal design with a nod to history and quality craftsmanship . . ."

The color palette is cool Scandinavian, mostly light blues and grays with some pastel shades. Lars tried to recreate the exact light blue that is used on the woodwork in the local farmhouses by mixing blue and light-gray paints. Linseed oil paints were used throughout and many of the floors are a light gray, creating a contrast to the unpainted wooden walls in some rooms. In the dining area where the walls are papered, the wooden floorboards have been left in their glorious natural state. However, Lars is not afraid to experiment with bold colors and he has incorporated some into the overall scheme: notably, a pink hallway with splatter paint and a bathroom with gold wallpaper. Surprisingly, these extravagant touches work and don't feel out of place. The kitchen, which is predominantly white and simplicity personified, blends a range of different styles, including old, new, used and custom-made. Thus the large minimalist stainless steel freezer manages to sit well with the old cupboard dating back to 1649.

Unfussy, neat and without any curtains, this is a cabin that has been furnished with great care and simplicity. The architecture, with its beautifully proportioned paned windows, is on show for all to see. The neat and finished wood cladding and linen wall panels echo these lovely proportions. Here, everything is simple but beautifully considered, and there is an orderliness and discipline of thought here. It's an arts and crafts hangout that is held together by a structured backbone of well-organized thought; a beautiful space that encourages contemplation.

ECO-CHIC CABINS

Joao Rodrigues has a busy, stressful life, running several businesses as well as working as an airline pilot, so it's not surprising that he wanted to create a retreat where he, his wife and four children, together with family and friends, could unwind and relax. However, what started as a project for a weekend home ended up as a small luxury holiday venue.

THE STRUCTURE

This project consists of four separate thatch-roofed huts – two made of wood and reeds, and two built from white concrete – with traditional sand and concrete floors. They are located among the sand dunes and rice paddies of a natural wildlife reserve near the small coastal fishing village of Carrasqueira, one hour's drive south of Lisbon. Joao wanted to create a group of traditional cabanas in the local minimalist style, where he could give his children the opportunity to savor new experiences and a sense of freedom in a safe environment where they could have fun and become more aware of the natural world. The area is home to a plethora of wildlife, including flamingos, storks and dolphins.

CHANGE OF PLAN

Working in close collaboration with his friend, architect Manuel Aires Mateus, Joao planned to build a cluster of ecologically sound huts, using only traditional materials and building techniques. The project was completed in just over a year and, to his great surprise, Casas na Areia was nominated to represent Portugal at the 2010 Venice Biennale International Architecture Exhibition, giving it global exposure. Indeed, there was so much interest that Joao decided to open the doors to the general public, and it quickly became fully booked.

MATERIALS AND BUILD

Only locally available natural materials – pine wood and reeds harvested on the banks of the nearby River Sado – were used in the build. Both Joao and Manuel were passionate about respecting regional traditions and building methods while reinterpreting them for modern use, and they commissioned Antonio Pinela, a local craftsman with age-old skills steeped in the history and heritage of the area, to construct the huts.

A major challenge was how to emulate the traditional sand floors of Portuguese cabanas to make them warm and comfortable underfoot all year-round – when sand gets cold in winter, it becomes hard and uncomfortable. Manuel was inspired after visiting a Tate Modern art installation by the Brazilian artist Cildo Meireles. He observed people walking across a room strewn with talcum powder, noting how the talc was distributed and how they were forced to slow down and consider their movement. He wanted to achieve the same effect in the cabanas. His solution was to create a cement surface with underfloor heating and to scatter a thick layer of sand on top. Once hot, it stays warm for up to two days.

With only a limited color palette and range of materials, these simple eco-cabins are really stunning. The structures are made of pine and reeds, while the interior furnishings are white and oversized like the pendant lamps, which emit a glowing spherical light over the large table and cast no shadow.

STYLE NOTES

These thatched beach huts are little self-contained havens of peace and tranquility. Inside, everything is calm and minimalist, reduced to life's bare essentials, albeit in a luxurious and high-end way. To create this feeling of comfort and simplicity, a neutral palette of natural and historical colors was used throughout. Inside two of the huts, the reed-lined walls have been left exposed with the supporting horizontal wooden beams also on show, and in the remaining cabanas the walls are painted uniformly white. The sand-covered floors look invitingly soft and textured with the trailing imprints of bare and shoe-clad feet. The sand symbolizes the unifying element between the internal and external worlds, linking the natural environment outside with the human interior and thereby transforming the space, enhancing its romance and changing our perceptions of its scale.

The usual high-tech communication and media gadgets have been installed in these simple cabanas – there's high-speed Internet and an iPod docking sound system. Nevertheless, life here is all about getting back to basics, disconnecting from the modern world and reconnecting with each other and with nature. You are forced to slow down – it's difficult to walk fast on sand and you have to adopt a different, more relaxing pace.

It's difficult to look at these interiors and not wish you were there, sitting on the huge white sofas and wiggling your toes in the warmed sandy floor. The bedrooms and bathrooms, too, are an exercise in balanced, minimal symmetry. The color palette is limited, the two bedside tables made of rough tree trunks adding texture and the wall-hung lights echoing the identical balance of the room. It's beautiful and calming.

"to make the sand floors warm and comfortable all year round, a cement surface with underfloor heating was created and a thick layer of sand was scattered on top. Once hot, it stays warm for up to two days . . ."

The cabanas have different functions: one is a communal open space with living, dining and kitchen areas, while the others consist of bedrooms and bathrooms. The simple furniture is completely unadorned and stripped right back to the natural wood or simply painted white. The relaxing squashy sofas are white, as are the lampshades and the bedcovers and linen curtains in the gleaming white bedrooms and bathrooms. While staying true to the original design and feel of traditional Portuguese fishermen's huts, the contemporary plumbing, floor-length windows and glass doors, and Corian kitchen counters all conform to the modern standards we now expect, as do the dishwasher, microwave oven and coffee machine.

Outside, the garden has been left deliberately wild, melding into the sandy dunes, and there's a small lap pool into which you can plunge for a refreshing swim on hot summer days before drying off and relaxing on the large daybed to watch a spectacular sunset. This really is a transforming place where you can escape the everyday pressures of modern life and just hang out with family and friends, chill and commune with nature.

RIVERBANK CABANAS

Cabanas No Rio was the second project for Joao Rodrigues (see page 100) following the commercial success and critical acclaim for Casas na Areia, which was originally designed as a family weekend retreat but evolved into an eco-friendly hotel. With a full-time job as a pilot, various business interests and a busy lifestyle, Joao wanted a laid-back place to unwind with his family and friends – where he and his wife could relax and his children could experience the natural world and have more freedom.

ARCHETYPAL FORMS

These two rustic 150 sq ft (14 sq m) cabins stand on the banks of the River Sado beside a picturesque small jetty on stilts. It's only a one-hour drive from Lisbon to the village of Comporta, set in a magnificent watery nature reserve. Across the water is the unique stilted palafitte harbor of Carrasqueira, a masterpiece of folk architecture. This fragile-looking port was an ingenious solution for the local fishing community, enabling them to access their boats during low tides when the riverbanks were muddy.

The actual forms are highly archetypal and each of these spaces has its own specific function. The first cabin consists of a bedroom with an en suite bathroom and an unusual shower that can be used outside as well as indoors. The second cabin is a living area with a small kitchen equipped for preparing and cooking simple meals.

INSPIRATION

The old cabanas had previously been fishermen's shacks and when Joao bought them he installed a few chairs so the family could just spend the day there relaxing. However, despite the lack of basic comforts and utilities, his children wanted to sleep there overnight, and he and his wife started thinking about what they would need to do to make staying there a pleasurable experience for the whole family.

RESPECTING LOCAL TRADITIONS

Working again with his friend the architect Manuel Aires Mateus, Joao's plan was to completely refurbish the fishing shacks and create a romantic refuge from the pressures of the modern world. They decided to achieve this by using and recycling local materials and respecting regional skills, crafts and traditions. They wanted to mirror the concept of the medieval palafitte wharf, which was constructed solely from wood. "Its identity has remained intact long beyond the material's resistance, enabling it to be changed and replaced while keeping all its original values intact."

The internal wooden surfaces reflect the materials used in the construction. The recycled local materials are so limited and simple that your eye is naturally drawn to the spectacular natural watery landscape outside. The four-sided angular roof creates a lofty feel, making the small interior space feel larger and more relaxing.

MATERIALS AND BUILD

The two cabanas are entirely finished in recycled local wooden panels, which are left exposed (both inside and out) to weather attractively with the passing of time and the seasons. They were built off-site in a carpenter's workshop and then transported on the back of a truck to their current location on the edge of the estuary with their own private deck and pontoon. Once the initial design had been completed, the project was relatively quick and easy to implement and the cabanas were ready in just over six months.

STYLE NOTES

Exuding calm and tranquillity, these cabanas are simply finished and furnished. Natural materials and a palette of neutral muted colors have been used to instill the space with a sense of simplicity, helping you to disconnect from the material world and to engage with nature. This place is really captivating – you can put all your worries and stress aside and have time to indulge yourself and to focus on the important things in life: family, friendship and love.

Nevertheless, despite the "otherworldly" feel, you aren't entirely cut off from the things we take for granted in the modern world; there's a Wi-Fi connection and an iPod docking station, but no television. You have to make your own amusements here. When you're not walking, swimming, cooking or just meditating, you can venture out across the estuary in the kayak "parked" beside the pontoon.

The roof of the bedroom was designed purposefully to be higher at the front than the back, making you feel protected and held safely within the building – it's reassuringly snug. As a contrast, in the living room in the other cabana, the incline of the ceiling gives you the sensation of being projected into the natural world outside. This clever design adds tension to each space, according to its function.

"the old cabanas had been fishermen's shacks and Joao installed a few chairs so the family could spend the day there relaxing, but, despite the lack of basic comforts and utilities, his children wanted to sleep there overnight . . ."

The furniture, though simple, is very stylish and doesn't overwhelm, blending seamlessly into the whole. The comfortable deep Gervasoni and Ghost armchairs covered in white linen are by Paola Navone, with side tables to match. The four-poster bed, swathed in white muslin with gleaming white pillows and bed covers, adds a touch of luxury but, again, it is constructed very simply with everything reduced to the unfussy, minimal basics. On hot summer days, the doors to the shower room can be thrown open wide, transporting you outside, whereas on colder days they can be closed to create a cozy, warm-toned space.

Decorative objects are kept to the bare minimum throughout: a traditional steel fan, a white table lamp and books. The lighting is warm yet subdued, and the wood-paneled walls almost make you feel cocooned – it's like being back in the womb. For Joao, this project "confirms the lost paradigm of life – that true happiness is based on the intelligent use of simplicity." And how right he is.

WORKSPACES

The small spaces featured in the following pages just go to prove that working environments, whether they're practical, creative or administrative, do not have to be large or in a traditional or urban location. No matter how quirky or seemingly remote, these cabins, studios and even a wrecked beach hut fulfill the job description for which they were designed and intended. They are all simple yet considered with their own strong aesthetic. As one of their creators and owners says: "Things that are made well to work well often look well."

There's a young emergency room nurse who discovered her talent and love for woodwork and transformed a shabby garden storeroom into a fully functioning workshop where she fashions beautiful items from discarded wood. In a simple wooden hut with a tin roof in the Cornish countryside, a craftsman and roofer has created a shelter he can use while working on the land, and it doubles up as an inspirational family space for his children, which requires them to develop their creativity and have fun making things.

The inventiveness of some people knows no bounds. On the north Norfolk coast a creative fellow has recycled the wood from a storm-wrecked beach hut to make a mobile vintage stall for a friend. Further along the same stretch of coastline, a skilled woodworking builder has constructed a multifunctional space that combines a home design studio/office with storage for his tools and materials. And a serial shed-building artist from Scotland has used salvaged scaffolding boards, recycled tin roofing and glass from a dismantled conservatory to build a special tree house with views over his garden and the surrounding countryside.

Over on the Scottish east coast is a busy functioning boat painters' workshop with a very unusual and colorful exterior. Over the decades, generations of skilled workmen have wiped the excess paint in their brushes over the exterior walls, creating an ever-changing abstract tableau. And continuing the theme of boats, a talented product and furniture designer in Auckland, New Zealand, has converted an old boathouse shed into a design studio and office, which is also used as a social space for entertaining friends on weekends.

WOODWORK STUDIO

One of those people whose talent, drive and achievements are in excess of their years is Sophie Heron. This young emergency room nurse with a big love for woodwork has a quiet inner strength. Along with creating a wood-based business for herself, she has now built her own backyard workshop/studio. She's as nice a person as she is genuinely cool, and you can't help but wish her well and watch her grow.

THE BUILD

Originally a shabby plywood garden storeroom for her landscape designer father's equipment and tools, the studio is located at the end of the garden of their family home. Here, Sophie's woodworking started off in a corner of the building and gradually took over. Together with her boyfriend and father, she built a 10 x 14 ft (3 x 4.5 m) extension at the back, which almost doubled the original size. They insulated it, added a floor and reclaimed windows, and clad the exterior with bargain vertical strips of palette wood from a wood recycling center. The roof is covered in black butyl pond liner left over from one of Sophie's father's jobs.

WORKING SPACE

The workshop is sited beneath a row of silver birch trees and the aspect to the front and back is good: at the rear, the window looks out over a neighbor's field where a horse grazes, while the view at the front is of the garden and the house. Sophie has moved outwards, too, in terms of her workspace: she usually leaves the door open while she's working, and an outdoor workbench is placed out front. Her plan was for it to resemble an old mill interior, with a wooden floor, white walls and maximum daylight. She wanted to keep the space really clean with everything in its own place.

A generous local farmer donated an old reclaimed maple parquet floor, and another kind friend gave her the potbellied stove, something Sophie feels has revolutionized the space. "I was trying to scrape a living. The old place had an electric heater but no insulation and it was freezing. I'd take my boots off and rest my toes between the rungs of the radiator . . . but now the stove is on every day, burning offcuts of wood I get for free."

Built using recycled and salvaged wood, this unassuming vertically clad studio is the base for Sophie's woodcarving business. Donated softwood is kept in the adjacent wood storage for burning on the stove.

"the old place had an electric heater but no insulation and was freezing . . . now the stove is on every day, burning free offcuts of wood . . ."

THE CREATOR

Sophie's amazing journey began simply, with the family deciding to take a step back from the usual big-spending Christmas in favor of a more homely, crafts-based celebration with only handmade presents. While her sister enjoyed crocheting and making soap, Sophie used her father's tools and some discarded palette wood to fashion a bird feeder, an apple store for her mother, some candleholders and chopping boards. She was hooked and the woodwork took hold of her. Between emergency room shifts she focused on her new passion and became more independent in her skills base. Everyone loved what she produced and she was making money and enjoying it. Watching online videos, she taught herself wood carving, buying the necessary tools from her nurse's wages, and embarked on the project of fitting out the spectacular wooden interior of her Volkswagen bus. She started selling her wares online and at craft shows and cut down her hours at the hospital to part-time working. Now, her work is expanding: she's posting her creations on Instagram, and making items for galleries, her website and craft shows. They include hand-carved kitchenware, spoons, scoops, plant holders, honey ladles and plant hangers – what Sophie calls "handmade goods with wood."

MATERIALS

Sophie uses all found, donated, recycled or salvaged wood, both for the workshop building itself and in her work. Outside her simple cabin are two wood stores, one containing pallet wood – softwood that she can't carve but which is used to heat the house and workshop – and the other stacked with the hardwoods she uses for her work. Her favorites are English walnut (from a storm-fallen tree), oak, cherry and maple. Each piece of wood comes with its own story, as does every item she carves. Growing up in the village, Sophie knows the local carpenter and farmers and talks to everyone she meets, so she often hears about and gets pieces of wood that nobody else wants. She even describes herself as "a bit of a skip [dumpster] rat," salvaging and carving useful wood from discarded items.

The studio interior is as orderly as you would expect from a former nurse. The tools are kept in neat racks, the place is swept, and the rug and houseplants add a sense of life and homeliness to this creative space.

STYLE NOTES

This is an attractive but practical workspace in which Sophie has created the atmosphere and space that she needs for her work. Most people who have received some professional, practically skilled and responsible training understand the need to be neat and orderly, to take care of your equipment and to be able to quickly put your hand on your work tools. This practical approach lets you focus on the task at hand. Combine that practicality and discipline with a creative talent, and you have a world of potential.

Sophie's workshop is light, airy and warm, a space where you could be happy. The horse in the field at the back often comes up to the workshop window in the evening, and she gives him the leftover apple core from her midmorning break. Decoratively, it is simple with the right balance, a practical space where you can work intensively, or just sit and be creative or hang out. Her hand-crafted items, plant holders and test pieces decorate the space, while some simple fairy lights from IKEA and a few potted plants provide the finishing touches. For Sophie, the workshop changed everything. As she puts it: "I have a place for storing all the things I make, which is light, warm and comfortable, and there's no way I could have built and developed the business without it." It has made her working life a pleasure.

SCOTTISH PAINTERS' SHACK

Rarely, but wonderfully when it happens, an absolutely functional building acquires a unique, unselfconscious visual character. Totally authentic and genuinely produced as a by-product of the fishing boat painting and signwriting business, the remarkable exterior of this workshop has accrued thick layers of colorful paint, which have been built up over a period of time by the skilled workmen wiping off the excess paint left in the bristles of their paintbrushes against the building's outer walls. This is no conscious or planned piece of artwork but it's equally beautiful to look at, appreciate and be inspired by.

THE BACKGROUND

The William B. Bruce ship painters' workshop occupies a building in the Scottish fishing town of Fraserburgh. It was founded in 1960 by William Buchan Bruce, the father of Fred, the current proprietor. The building is a functional space: a long brick-built structure with a pebble dash finish and a sloping roof of profile sheeting. It's a practical working space, which was never intended to be decorative, and it's divided longitudinally into units, occupied by the ship painters. Consistency is a feature of the workforce, too. The firm employs up to 20 people, including Fred's two sons, and the workers are mostly full-time painters, along with some seasonal staff. Many of them are naturally talented in certain areas, and some of the employees started work here straight from school and have been employed here all their lives. Most of the painters are trained on the job, acquiring their skills as they work, alongside other employees who are certified to carry out specific tasks.

Built up over 60 years of accumulated paint from the ship painters cleaning their brushes on the exterior of the building, the paint has morphed into unintended artfully thick layers of an abstract, dripping, multicolored mass. The painters' workshop is adjacent to the "ship lift," where the boats are lifted out of the water for repainting and repairs.

The workshop is sited adjacent to the "ship lift," where the boats are lifted up out of the water to undergo repairs, such as their annual repainting, in the open air. From their base, the ship painters go out each day to paint the fishing boats, which vary in size from 33 to 108 ft (10 to 33 m) in length, although much larger boats are painted when they are out of the water and in the dry dock. Fishing for whitefish, shellfish and pelagic fish, such as herring, the smaller vessels trawl the North Sea waters and the west coast of Scotland while the larger boats venture further afield. And outside of the fishing fleet, the William B. Bruce ship painters also ply their trade to the local ferries as well as the oil rig supply vessels.

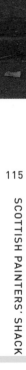

UNINTENTIONAL ART

Specialist marine coatings are used for painting specific areas of the boats, colored according to their owners' preferences, and the accumulated paint on the exterior walls has been built up gradually over a period of 60 years as the painters used them for cleaning their brushes and rollers. The ship painters' brushes are mostly pure bristle, varying in size from large to very small dependent on each specific task, and along with the brushes they also use paint rollers.

As far as the painters know, the paint buildup is unique to this building and a practice specific to this company. The men who work here are so accustomed to it that they don't really notice it anymore or share the fascination of us outsiders. It's the passersby who stop and stare and take the pictures. The men's focus is on their work – from 8 a.m. to 5 p.m. every day with an hour for lunch and two 20-minute tea breaks. Theirs is hard and dirty work – painting, cleaning, scrubbing, scraping, washing and sweeping.

Little has changed here over time. In the same way that the mass of paint has accrued on the exterior, the typeface used on the ships is unchanged. Hand-painted signwriting is a skill not often seen these days, and the signwriters at this yard have a specific house style of typeface that they have always used, although they can accommodate different styles as requested by owners.

STYLE NOTES

This unique 3-D surface stops you in your tracks, and reminds you how the world around us is full of suprising, inspiring and beautiful things, albeit often in unexpected ways. Here, totally unselfconsciously, the ships' painters have cleaned the excess paint from their brushes, over many years, on the exterior walls of their workplace, and the result is a strongly colored, roughly textured mass of paint. It looks almost geological in form, like stalagmites growing up inside a cave, or the deeply layered resin emanating from tree bark. Nature here is man's hand, tradition, practicality and, no doubt, for the first painter to have daubed the wall, a touch of rebelliousness, too.

BOATHOUSE DESIGN OFFICE

Jamie McClellan, a respected product and furniture designer, lives in New Zealand and, along with his work, he loves bicycles and sailing. He is so obsessed with boats and being close to the water that he transformed an old boathouse shed into a simple but stylish design studio.

JAMIE'S STUDIO

Jamie's practice is fast becoming known as the go-to product design studio for considered and consistently thoughtful three-dimensional design. As he says, "We're lucky to have a really diverse range of clients whose vision aligns with ours. We get to work with lots of really clever people, from those producing world-beating sports equipment to start-ups taking on the world." Keeping him company in the studio is Walnut, his border terrier – "a perfect little mix of rough 'n' tumble and affection. Fast enough to chase me on my bike down the cycle path and yet small enough to fit in a backpack when we need to weave through traffic."

WORKING BY THE WATER

Jamie had long hankered after one of these boathouse sheds. His friend Gideon Bing, an artist who worked in one of the boathouses, contacted him when the one next door became vacant. "He knew that I'd love to work in one of the sheds and we pounced!" The shed is located on the Orakei Basin, only a few minutes from downtown Auckland. The boathouses are almost 100 years old and of timber construction, clad with fiber panels and tiles, and set on concrete piles into the seabed below. The interior is lined with whitewashed marine ply on the floor, whitewashed rough sawn timber on the walls, and white painted tongue and groove on the ceiling.

The specific nature of the location means that the light, wind and water play a key part in creating the atmosphere. "The shed is southwest facing, and we get the sun late in the day – the sunsets are spectacular."

Previously Jamie had worked in a large downtown warehouse, a shared space with three other businesses, and although he liked it, the idea of having his own more private space was very appealing – plus the bonus of being able to work and spend his day beside the water he loves. Before

moving in here he had developed "a routine of stopping by the water on my cycle to work to think about and plan the day ahead. Being as close as possible to sea level on a daily basis has become an indispensable part of my being." And this informs his work and his design philosophy.

His sailboat, *Quick Nik,* is berthed just five minutes away in the marina across the road; any nearer would be far too much of a distraction. As Jamie says, "Sailing boats can't fit under the bridge that connects the causeway and creates the basin, which is probably a very good thing, as if there's not enough distraction out front already!"

GOING OUT TO WORK

Although working away from home may not be considered a benefit by many people with a difficult commute to work, there are some important benefits of having a separate workplace. As Jamie explains: "Separation for me is important. Partly it's just being in an environment where you can make a mess and have all your tools, samples, references and inspirations easily at hand. However, I also think that the routine of going somewhere to work is important to me. I have been commuting on a bike to work for more than a decade now and I feel incomplete without my daily cycle."

DESIGN PHILOSOPHY

Jamie may not be a great fan of styling, but he's massively keen on form, and his work has a purity and simplicity born out of thought and consideration. He particularly loves items that have a strong silhouette, believing his design should be "an object distilled down to the purest, calmest and most efficient form but often with a key detail that's expressed with confidence – visually balanced, a celebration of engineering, not an ounce of 'styling.' Everything should be in its right place, and with a purpose." Jamie's philosophy and use of the space were equally clear and purposeful: just to get into it and then enjoy every minute. He gets a lot of use out of the shed, beyond just working in it. He often entertains and has dinner parties and social gatherings, and it's also a lovely spot for a morning coffee and brunch at weekends.

"Whilst it's not really a project but more a transition, moving into the boat shed has felt like something we were always meant to do. And looking back now, it feels obvious that we'd end up here. There are magic times of the day when the light is reflecting off the water in a particular way, the sun is just right and the tide is perfectly high. Throw in a visiting seal pup or a leaping fish, and you can't help but laugh at how ridiculously lucky we are to have this as our office space."

STYLE NOTES

As this was an existing build, the studio didn't need a lot of fitting out and was more or less ready to go. "A cooking show had been filmed here and the kitchen was a series of mobile units on castors. We cut these down and shifted them against the wall. And aside from installing our own furniture, we didn't have to do much else. We replaced the scaffolding deck out front and painted it charcoal . . . and we've put up a flagpole."

The transparent plastic roller shutter acts as a window and large garage door facing the water, but at some point Jamie would like to replace it with bifold doors. Apart from that there's a "hobbit door" on the street side and a series of skylights. An area of the floor also opens up to the water, which is especially thrilling when there's a spring tide and the difference in the height of the water is evident. It makes Jamie think about rising sea levels: "It will be interesting to see how long it takes before we need to think about lifting the shed up a foot or so on its piles – I read recently that it could be 10 ft (3 m) in 50 years, which is alarming."

When it comes to style, Jamie's preference is for a simple space in which the objects are the heroes. This makes sense, reflecting his character, his ideas, and his profession. "I am, after all, a product and furniture designer. Our goal when we took over the shed was to keep it as clean as possible. We were worried that it might be too rustic, not gallery-esque enough, but actually the rustic nature has lent itself well to our sometimes less-than-clinical design practices." For instance, the cork stool by Jasper Morrison is "a great little companion to the black Lumber Chair. It just fits so nicely with the timbers and tones elsewhere, and completes my special spot to sit and reflect, no matter the weather."

The central table and chairs are by Michael Draper, while the Vitra chairs were brought here from Jamie's previous office space. "The large mahogany table was designed to suit the shed and it has since gone on to have a life of its own as a production piece, available in a number of sizes and timbers. The black Elementary chairs that accompany the table were designed for an Australian client and they seemed a good fit within the space, so we ordered a bunch of them."

121

BUILDER'S DESIGN STUDIO

Living on the North Norfolk coast, John is a builder working with timber. For him, the process is all about wood, from the seedling right through to something beautifully made. He works with large-dimension timber, principally locally sourced green oak, in partnership with his son from a studio he built himself. Functioning as a practical space for his work, it's an office, store and home workshop. The large-scale construction work happens in a modern industrial unit several miles away. John built this structure with the simple aims of having a store for his tools and materials plus a little office rather than working out of a study at home.

THE BUILD

Built as a painted timber structure that would fit seamlessly into this natural, coastal landscape in the style of a small agricultural building, this cabin has a soft wood timber frame. It's clad with robustly sized feather-edged boarding, and the exterior is painted with a water-based paint. The office is 16 ft (5 m) long, 13 ft (4 m) wide and 10 ft (3 m) tall. The adjoining workshop and store are a bit bigger. The roof is tiled with reclaimed curvy-ridged, deep red local handmade Norfolk clay pantiles.

Its purpose is clear: it's a conveniently located, simply designed and well-functioning build. John sums it up: "This building works well for us: we can be warm and work out how to build things in a fairly neutral space away from home distractions. The house is a short distance away through the garden, and the adjacent workshop allows for a little experimenting with materials as well as some fun making things."

ANCIENT AND MODERN

The window openings are mixed: either large panes of glass or an older metal-framed industrial style. John has a special technique that he likes to use for overglazing in oak-frame buildings: "We place the glass on the exterior of the wooden frame, sealed with foam rubber gasket tape, and then overlay a simple wooden frame to secure the double-glazed pane in place. It allows you to glaze a building without making window joinery first. I bought the small metal window in a farm sale in Denmark. I thought I might use it one day and, sure enough, it was just the job for making the most of the big view across the fields."

EXTERIOR FINISH AND FEATURES

The color of the exterior is RAL 7030, a code originally used by the German state commission but now a EU-wide classification, and nicknamed by John "carpenter's pouch." On one wall, a rusty, elegant and elongated letter "J" is fixed. It's John's initial, but in the past it was a nod to a former builder with the same initial and it served a practical purpose, too. This 200-year-old wrought-iron letter would have been fixed to the gable end of a stone building on the outside with a rod through the wall that would fix to the roof structure. This was known as a purlin strap and it secured the roof and gable together. Builders would use their initials to leave their mark, or sometimes numerals to indicate the date of the building.

The two roughly hewn chairs outside were made as experimental functional sculptural pieces by John's son Frank with a chain saw. And above the double workshop doors is the tip of a sperm whale's jaw that was washed up on the local coast – it's 3 ft (1 m) long. This is a flat world of big, fast-moving skies and wide horizons that open up your sight lines, creating an expanded visual frame. With such an enveloping atmosphere and natural color palette, it's no surprise that John says, "The landscape and big skies outside offer us so much, so we deliberately chose a muted warm color that often reflects what's going on out there."

John designed the interior space so that wherever he's working, at the drawing board or his desk, he has a framed view of the land outside. The wooden stools under the desk were locally made from oak and fir.

OUTSIDE

Beautifully neat stacks of wood outside the studio help to ground the building in its purpose and locality. John explains that these wood piles are "offcuts from our work with green oak and they need to dry out before they're ready to be used for firewood. This method of stacking came about from several influences. A local gamekeeper told me that the best way to dry wood is out in the open where the sun can shine on it and the wind can move round it – not thrown into a shed under cover in a green state."

His love of stacking things neatly and elegantly runs deep. "When I was a child, I enjoyed lots of holidays in County Kerry in Ireland and we used to get involved in stacking turf [peat], a fuel that my uncles and aunts would dig, dry and collect from the bog. In large collections it was stacked into a reek, which was more elongated than the stacks I build but looked lovely and was very functional. So I gave it a go and made these stacks in a similar way, and they work well as a drying shape. Butterflies and big bumblebees live out the winter inside them. I've seen similar huge storage stacks of wood in Sweden and Poland."

And the delightfully rusting vintage French Citroën H van parked outside is the firm's former mobile works tearoom, which John used to drive from site to site and job to job when he was still a general builder. The plan now is to sell this beauty as a restoration job.

THE INTERIOR

John's plan was to create an interior that was simply finished and needed no decorating, and he lined it with birch-faced plywood. Part of his design philosophy addresses the inherent relationship between true beauty and functionality. Put simply: "Things that are made well to work well often look well." The vintage industrial-looking drawing board at which he works is an antique Nike Eskilstuna model from Sweden, and it has a hydraulic mechanism that allows for smooth adjustments. He bought it from a house clearance man who thought it was a tire-fitting machine. It must have been the doyen of drawing boards in its day.

Whether he works at the board or his desk, the design process for John depends on the level of the inquiry and scale of the job, ranging from the design of a home studio to collaborating with architects and engineers in a larger scale oak-frame design for a new build. The interior space was laid out accordingly, and the windows were placed carefully. Wherever John works inside, there's a framed view of the exterior landscape. "The layout, with low-level fixed desks, allows for a space for a computer and keyboard by the little iron window with the big view. And the desk area under the large fixed window, which is north facing, is ideal for unfolding plans and doing general paperwork." On the other side of the office, with the large clear wall space, there's a drawing board by the window, so John can even work out his ideas standing up.

The functional working features of the studio are decorative, too. Carefully chosen by John are some vintage European pieces, including the angular, modernist desk light known as a Walligraph lamp and manufactured by Walter Grafton of Eltham, London, in the 1920s – "an overlooked British design that is equal to the Bauhaus designs of the same period." The 1970s wood burner has Scandinavian roots, and its door, when fully open, can slide underneath to allow for an open fire; it's a great functional design.

The chrome desk light is by Hadrill and Horstmann and was made with an integral magnifying glass that was used by dental technicians and opticians. Anyone working at a desk understands that your posture affects both you and your work, and John prefers the uprightness that a stool naturally encourages. The two turned wood stools were made locally and inspired by a design by Russell Pinch. They are fashioned from local oak and Douglas fir, which were sourced from a local firewood dealer. The cream gloss–painted chair with the over-large backrest set against the plan-covered birch ply wall is one of a set that John bought in Ireland. "Carpenter's chairs were made in rural Ireland by local carpenters who copied the proper English ones in the houses of their landlords. So they didn't always get the proportions right and many tend to be heavy. They are made of ash and have a low seat to keep you below the smoke of the open turf fires which often used to seep into the room."

STYLE NOTES

Filling that perfect space between too much and too little, this studio/office has been designed by and for its owner. By figuring out exactly what he needs in terms of the equally important big elemental features and the small details, and balancing the two, he has made it work for him, creating the right atmosphere, level of comfort and creative stimulus. It's light and warm – the large windows and wood burner see to that. And, as a bonus, it stands only about 100 yd (90 m) from his home, which must be the most perfect commutable distance ever.

The desk height, stool height and design are right for John. The desk light not only serves its purpose but is a design feature and an inspiration, too. The carpenter's chair also comes with a story that influences its design, and the vintage drawing board is absolutely beautiful, functional and reflects the family's Nordic and European roots. In summary, this functional design studio and workshop is about as simple and considered as you can get without going anywhere near the road of big spends.

SIMPLE CABIN

Ben Verry is a modern craftsman and roofer working with passion and the most time-honored materials to keep old building traditions alive. He uses scantle slate, a style of roofing made with differing sizes of slate tiles that is rarely found outside of Wales and Cornwall. The hut he created is a simple space of wooden construction with a tin roof. It's welcoming and homely, somewhere he can use as a shelter while working his land, and which also offers what many of us dream of: a place of sanctuary and escape.

CONNECTING WITH NATURE

Ben had always wanted his own land and when the opportunity arose to buy some he decided to build a shelter, which he could use when working and managing the land. It also served as a place for visiting friends and family to escape bad weather. He uses the hut as his personal workshop – somewhere he can create and make things as well as rest or brew cups of tea. His children, too, love this space; it's part of the natural world and great outdoors where they can make dens and just play. Off-grid, this is a family space where you can connect with nature and escape the modern world and technology – the iPads are left at home.

Over the past decade or so the land has been transformed into a wood with well over 800 trees planted on the site, including alder – a fast-growing hardwood that Ben uses for making charcoal and logging – along with larch, yew, ash and oak trees.

THE BEFORE AND AFTER – BUILT FROM SCRATCH

It was important to Ben that the space fitted into the landscape, visually and environmentally. Using natural materials, this is a temporary structure, built to be ecologically sound with as little impact on the environment as possible. The project took six months from start to finish with the final construction and assembly stage on-site accomplished in just three days, albeit with a large group of friends and family providing assistance and manpower. Grateful for their help, Ben feels that he owes them a lot and the value of their friendship wasn't lost on him. This was a team effort.

The site for the shelter was uneven and Ben created a stilt-like frame to create a level surface on which to build. The structure itself was made off-site in his workshop in sections measuring 13 x 6 ft 6 in (4 x 2 m). They were transported to the site on a trailer and then bolted together.

MATERIALS AND UTILITIES

The base of this little building sits on dock timber stilts, and the decking consists of recycled scaffold planks. The internal walls are made from plywood while the external cladding is sweet chestnut. The windows are old double-glazed units that were found in a dumpster, and the roof is a section of tin. To reduce the impact of the building, Ben kept the pitch of the roof low, which helped to reduce its height. The tin roof was quick and easy to fix in place after the building sections were bolted together. Dealing with the need for basic utilities without impacting the surrounding area, Ben started to dig out the compost toilet and then followed up by installing some small solar panels for charging a 12 v battery. Inside the cabin there are some simple comforts, including a small gas stove for boiling water for tea, and a wood burner for warmth. In winter, the water supply is a natural spring, which flows on the land, but this dries up in summer and fresh water has to be brought to the site on every visit.

OBJECTS AND FURNITURE

The furniture, including two small sofas, a table, chair and storage boxes, has mostly been donated. The tools were found at local car trunk sales. Ben and the children use them for making and mending things for friends, shaping wooden bits and pieces and creating sculptures. Above all, this is a creative space, and the children love to collect leaves, wood and clay and to use them to make things and create maps of this little piece of nature.

Daylight is key to making this simple wooden interior a comfortable space to be in. Long worktop surfaces were built below the large picture window to make full use of the light and the aspect. Food is brought up to the cabin and water is collected from a nearby spring.

"off-grid, this is a creative and inspiring family space where you can connect with nature and escape the modern world and technology – the iPads are left at home . . ."

THE FINISHED SPACE

This project hinged on the ability to make the sectional pieces off-site for ease of construction. Reducing the hut's impact on the location was key to Ben's ecological principles. Despite considering the environment in the actual build, dealing with it once the building had been constructed brought a whole new set of challenges, because nature decided it liked it too and a swarm of hornets moved in. Ben needed to move out temporarily while the infestation was sorted out, but then he had to figure out how to stop the insects from burrowing into the bark-faced wood cladding. Now, with the bark removed, that issue has been solved.

This simple space works well for all the members of Ben's family. He can work on the land while his children are fortunate enough to experience the freedom and great adventure that nature provides as well as life itself, distilled into its elemental parts: water, light, warmth and shelter. As Ben neatly describes it, "When you live simply you don't need much power. All you really need is some light. This space is such a quiet sanctuary and a refuge for us all. It sits peacefully within its environment and we can visit whenever we want. It's a space that inspires and motivates me to be creative."

RECYCLED BEACH HUT

Pete is a creative fellow, an artist and sculptor who works in many media, of which his favorites are plastic, wood, stone and steel. The pieces he creates are individual and full of character: huge driftwood spiders and circular woven hanging chairs made out of discarded fishermen's rope, as well as his own clifftop retreat and a mobile vintage shop for his friend and neighbor Karen, which is made from locally salvaged wood from storm-wrecked beach huts. His creativity is clearly backed up with great practical skills, learned along the way via the "university of life." At school he spent his time in the art, woodwork and metalwork departments, and his first job was for a blacksmith working on listed historical buildings. He moved on to an "inventive" employer with an amazing workshop, followed by a spell in the car refinishing trade. He was adding skills of working with different materials along the way and finding solutions to a range of challenges. "Life is all about solving problems. It's one big challenge, an obstacle course, but no matter how large the problem is, it can always be solved."

BACKGROUND

Some winters bring severe weather to the east coast of England, and storm surges caused by extremely high tides and brutally strong winds can damage coastal areas and properties. When the westerly longshore drift brought the wreckage of brightly colored beach huts to the local shoreline, Pete, helped by his nine-year-old son, joined in the community effort to clean up the beach. Every night they could be found on the shore, salvaging pieces of wood and stacking them up into a pile. There was a two-week window of opportunity to get the beach cleared, as a follow-up surge was expected, so they collected the wood quickly, creating a huge heap before denailing, sorting and stacking it in sizes and lengths.

Initially, Pete had no specific plan in mind, but one soon emerged and he decided to build Karen a mobile market stall from the debris. His idea was to create a small market cart that could be wheeled out during the day, then folded down and locked up at night.

MATERIALS, DESIGN AND CONSTRUCTION

The sheer quantity of salvaged material meant that Pete's vague idea could expand. He had enough materials to handcraft a small mobile building rather than a simple market stall, and from the quantity and lengths of debris available he knew that this build would need an idiosyncratic shape. These were no long regular lengths of wood – being storm-torn and wrecked they were irregular and randomly sized, all more or less the same width but with no really long pieces. Pete needed to use the available lengths and piece everything together to create a usable space; it was "a bit of a pick n' mix." Rather courageously, the design was to be completely free-form. A rough sketch was all the formality it needed; the rest of it came from Pete's head as he went along.

The beach huts originally stood on sturdy wooden railway sleepers. By splitting them with a chainsaw, Pete built the base carriage structure. The metal axles were crafted from old steel railings found on the beach. Pete built the display shelves for the shop early on, working outwards from the frame. And by creating angled sides to accommodate the shelving, no internal space was lost and the form of the exterior soon began to take shape.

The design followed on in the same vein. If the walls were going to be irregular and angular, then the roof would have to continue along similar lines. The shape of the hut evolved from the mental image Pete had of the beach huts left in a crumpled heap by the storm. He started to fill in the irregular shelf/framework shape using strips of wood in the appropriate lengths. The windows were whatever he had salvaged from the beach. The only purchased materials were the fixings, nails, bolts, roofing felt and insulation. Everything else came from the beach. For the roof covering he used colored shingles, each hand cut.

The amazing colored timber and roof shingles all came from storm-damaged local beach huts. The irregular lengths of wood lent themselves to a free-form build, and shorter pieces were cut into lengths to use as roofing shingles – nothing was wasted.

STYLE NOTES

Built over three months from storm-wrecked beach huts, Pete describes his multicolored, almost armadillo-like creation as "a happy building." It has a spirit. Each angle of the 23 x 5 ft (7 x 1.5 m) structure intrigues the eye. Its colors make sense and feel at home in this coastal location, while its idiosyncratic form feels free and angular yet organic. It's a triumph of nature and man's handiwork. Without Pete's eye and talent, the combination of natural and human forces, and the unexpected source of materials and qualities and inspiration they offered, this building would never have happened. Its design outside of its circumstances would seem beautiful but arbitrary, whereas in context it makes perfect sense. It is intriguing, engaging the eye and demanding attention.

STUDIOS & WORKSHOPS

All artists and creative types yearn for a workspace of their own, however small. Light, atmosphere, basic comforts and practicalities outweigh luxury and a big budget. The most important consideration is that the space inspires you to be creative. Many of the studios featured have been built with recycled materials or fashioned out of unprepossessing, demolished or abandoned structures – they are thrifty as well as ecologically sound.

The artist Tessa Fahey wanted a special space for painting that was all her own, and built a studio in her garden in rural Norfolk. This restful place gives her a sense of freedom – to think through new ideas and be inspired. Another artist, Karen Luchtenstein, erected an abandoned 1960s "prefab" classroom in the backyard of her London home and transformed it into an adaptable space. As well as a studio, it's "a holiday" home away from home. Amanda Bannister set out to create a space in her back garden for her family to practice their arts and crafts and nurture their creative talents. The result is an intelligently designed studio, which doubles as a home office and guest bedroom. And despite its multifunctional purpose, it's a surprisingly tidy space, radiating calm and order with everything in its place.

On the windswept Scottish coast is another example of an art studio, specifically designed to connect the rich interior world of the artist with its unique wilderness location. Another Scottish artist, Peter McClaren, needs natural light to work – lots of it – so he created a studio where he could enjoy a "plein air experience indoors" by ingeniously recycling a stash of glass panes from local bus shelters. Inspired by the light, he says it's "like adding 100 new colors to your palette." On a steep green hillside in Devon a self-taught young artist and shed devotee built a rustic shed from scratch on the back of a truck, as well as a land-based studio shed. For Rob, owning at least one shed is a necessity, and he declares that "people with sheds live longer." He has all the zealous ardor and enthusiasm of the true believer.

A rotating observatory, used as a temporary blind for watching the bird life on the surrounding salt marsh and mud flats, is also a solitary studio for an artist in residence. Designed and built with impeccable environmental principles, it's an inviting space that engages the local community. On an "ecology island" in a neglected corner of a town in Kent, an extraordinary project was conceived for a communal educational resource that combined an arts and crafts studio and birdwatching blind. The result is colorful, dynamic and truly adventurous.

TESSA'S BACK GARDEN STUDIO

In the old orchard at the back of artist Tessa Fahey's Norfolk home stands her studio, an elegant blue-painted, weatherboarded, double-fronted structure with a traditional Norfolk tiled roof and a veranda running along the front. Tessa's husband, John, an architectural carpenter, built this large art-filled cabin for her on-site. Their long-term plan is to transition from the main house and eventually move up into the garden to build a new home there. This is their first step in that direction.

HISTORY AND EVOLUTION

John built the 19 x 16 ft (6 x 5 m) studio with softwood and cladding about 20 years ago on the site of a former tree house and old stable. Its original purpose was a place to keep tools and to use as a small workshop. Over the years it has had many uses – John and Tessa's son lived there for a while before it became her painting studio. Originally she used to paint in an upstairs room in the family house, but she always yearned for her own special space and having one gives her a sense of freedom – there are no telephones, no Internet. Every day she hears herself saying, "Let's go to the cabin," and this is an invitation to her friends and family to share and join in the creative and artistic experience.

The studio is surprisingly large inside, with several areas where Tessa and her friends can work. With doors and windows with two different aspects and roof lights, the natural light for working is good throughout the day. The blue 1960s chair is the prime spot for relaxing in front of the stove.

A SHARED SPACE

Inspired by her Swedish heritage, Tessa painted her studio a restful blue. A straight graveled path leads up a slight incline from the back of the house, which is partially hidden by hedges, so it feels separate with its own identity. Every day she brings her two flasks, one of coffee and the other of herbal tea, and sits in the 1960s blue vinyl swivel chair by the fire. She puts on some music or starts pacing up and down, thinking through the work for that day. Scraps of wood from John's work as a carpenter are used to light the antique wood-burning stove.

Wednesday mornings are an open studio here, where two friends, fellow local women artists, come and share the space, making coffee, working together, developing ideas, and inspiring and critiquing each other's work. However, for the rest of the week this is Tessa's studio, although she considers it an "open door," a shared space where people can come to talk and think through ideas. Tessa likes to walk up and down – it's her preferred means of developing an idea, and if it's still unclear, she sits and thinks by the Danish stove. There's a large north-facing skylight above the flat file, which she uses as a cutting table for her collage projects, and a large easel for her paintings. Her preferred style is abstraction but, as she says, "Sometimes I make myself be more specific."

139

STYLE NOTES

Paint, color and life are the three key elements to this studio interior. The painted floor is worn down by the passage of feet, while the exterior, the interior details and even the teapot are sources of painterly color inspiration, each contributing their small part towards creating an environment that is visually rich and conducive to creativity. It is an atmospheric space, with collected pieces adding graphic flashes. The stove, the rich blue 1960s swivel chair, the yellow vinyl-topped stool and the old kitchen dresser each tell their own story, adding color, texture and a comfortable, unpreciousness to this simple space.

"Tessa, inspired by her Scandinavian heritage, painted her studio a restful blue. Every day she brings two flasks, one of coffee and one of herbal tea, and sits in the 1960s blue vinyl swivel chair by the fire . . ."

Although this is primarily Tessa's domain, the cabin is communal, a shared space in the history of its usage within the family as well as one that friends love to visit to experience and enjoy its beautiful calm, thoughtful and creative mood. Such is that feeling that Tessa's husband, John, even knocks on the door before entering. It has a good balance of inward richness, art, books, music, places to sit, read or paint, and an openness towards the outdoors. The skylight illuminates the interior and even on rainy days the veranda provides a sheltered space where you can enjoy being outside in the fresh air. It isn't overdesigned or particularly self-conscious; it's a collated assembly of furniture, materials, textures, sources of inspiration and pieces of art. The creative force emerges not only from the people but also from the atmosphere, from the elements and the unique space that Tessa has curated.

THE OBSERVATORY

Close to the Hampshire Georgian coastal town of Lymington and near the Solent Way long-distance coastal pathway, the Observatory sits within the Lymington-Keyhaven Nature Reserve, an area of salt marsh and mud flats and a sanctuary for bird life. It consists of two demountable, rotating lookout shelters and a space for a series of artist's residencies. Many shed-like structures are solitary places, and although this has the capacity to be used as an art studio for a single artist, it engages the community in the widest sense – in both its creation and how it's used.

THE BACKGROUND

This project came about by means of a competition, working through a collaborative approach between different disciplines – artists, architects, engineers and students. Backed by a comprehensive education engagement program, the SPUD Group, which is a charitable foundation, has an impeccable track record for creating extraordinarily beautiful, individual spaces that engage with nature, the environment and the community. The group's purview integrates design, education, community involvement and art, engaging people of all ages. The Observatory is an addition to their accomplished series of projects, including the Exbury Egg.

A COLLABORATIVE EFFORT

Beginning with a design competition, the winning scheme proposed two rotating temporary buildings, each with strikingly angular shapes. They come with an air of mystery and at first sight it's not clear what they are, or what their function is. The idea was that this would be a place for people to look in and look out, and it would connect with the environment and the artist in residence. Environmentally sound principles would be applied, including collecting rainwater for the tap and sink while wastewater would be stored in a tank and disposed of when full.

On the design team were Charlotte Knight, Mina Gospavic, Ross Galtress and Lauren Shevills, four young architecture graduates who currently work at Feilden Clegg Bradley Studios, plus the Devon-based artist Edward Crumpton, who provided the insight into the working requirements of a contemporary artist. His art uses traditional British rope-weaving techniques, and this skill was integrated into the design to reference the coastal location and marine character of the build.

Other disciplines were engaged, each bringing specialist skills to the design. Structural and mechanical engineers and a cost engineer were called in to contribute their knowledge base and ensure that the design was practicable and feasible. As Mark Drury of SPUD says: "Everyone had to work really hard together to bring this project to fruition. Without all the people and partners involved none of it would have happened. They are as

much a part of the project as the project is part of its environment."

The collaborative principles by which SPUD operates are threaded through the entire design, build process and beyond. The timber merchants and construction companies offered both sponsorship and their extensive knowledge and expertise. The engineering, which is largely unseen within the Observatory structure, allows each pod to rotate through 360 degrees and doubles as a trailer for transportation purposes.

A CREATIVE SPACE

The aim was to make the Observatory a sculptural installation: a demountable and movable shelter, and a relocatable space. The plan was to move it to four locations over a period of time and to run an educational outreach program in each place. The build set out to create a peaceful atmosphere – a therapeutic space where artists could interact with the landscape and develop a body of work connected to each place within its context.

"the striking black exterior finish was created by using the process of *shou sugi ban* (charring wood). It's a natural way to preserve wood and to make it fire resistant . . ."

TRANSPORTABILITY

The Observatory is transportable, but for this concept to work it was important to make it achievable within the agreed budget plus it had to be simple and without any fuss. This objective was made even more challenging by factoring in the capacity for the structure to be demountable and transportable even to seemingly inaccessible locations off the beaten track where roads run out and the terrain becomes rough and uneven. Each member of the team brought their own particular specialist skills to the project to achieve this goal.

The challenge of transportability was eventually solved by the team of skilled engineers, who designed a special structure with a metal framework underneath, which doubled as a trailer. This enabled the building to be hitched up on wheels, along with a tow bar, and moved. Once it reaches the road it can be lifted on to a truck by means of a crane and transported over long distances to the next location.

MATERIALS
AND FINISHES

There are two structures. One is open to the elements for the public and visitors to use as a shelter, while the other is a closed glass structure for the resident artist. The exterior is principally built of larch whereas the interior is lined with Accoya wood, a fast-growing sustainable pine that is soaked in acetylated fluids (vinegars) to make it hard and preserve it. The frames were made from Tricoya wood, while marine plywood was also used within the building.

The striking black exterior finish was created by using the process of *shou sugi ban* (charring wood). This is a natural way to preserve wood and make it fire resistant, as well as preventing the potential for insect infestation. It gives the structure a beautiful finish and is a sustainable and environmentally friendly way of preserving without using chemicals. The char is only in the top ⅕ in (5 mm) on one side of the wooden surface. The carbonization gives it a carbonized glow, which picks up reflections of the light, the water, the sky, and the grass. A matte organic sealant is used as a final finish to stop the black from transferring. The woods are being tested using the *shou sugi ban* process to discover the long-term effects. One wall in each structure is made from a different wood in order to test the difference over the next two years. The interior furniture, too, is mostly made from the same woods.

STYLE NOTES

The striking black silhouettes of these buildings sit well within their location. Contrasting with natural light, black is a surprisingly good color outdoors. It juxtaposes with the natural environment, rendering the dark color, which you might think almost offensively out of place, perfect here. These two textural, angular structures are intriguing but beautifully at home, too. They are buildings that have been designed to engage with the outdoors, to rotate with the view and the light, while the studio physically insulates you but enables you to stay longer to look closer.

Each structure has a different atmosphere. The studio space is warm, quiet and secure inside, and when the doors are shut it feels cocoon-like. It's a fabulous place to sit in the dryness and warmth while being part of the outdoors, too. There's a vintage lamp and a charcoal heater with a narrow chimney, and as a place to work the outlook doesn't get much more inspiring. Due to the widening shape towards the glass door, your vision is steered and expanded out to the landscape where the tides rise and fall, and the sky and the light are changing constantly. The other space, however, is more open – it's just you and the elements. The wind whips through and the ropes flap about, so you're physically more involved with the environment.

Both structures can be cranked around on a central wheel, and with quite a bit of effort you can change your outlook from the studio, or face the other building away from the wind if you want. Although they look like remote "retreats," you're actually beside one of the many paths that crisscross the marshes. There's often someone on the horizon or strolling past walking their dog, birdwatching or cycling. People like to stop and chat, and have a look around the spaces. In practice, the design brief has been achieved; they are both really communal, sociable and inviting.

LONDON ARTIST'S BACKYARD STUDIO

Along with her other interests – interiors, history and lurchers – painting is the big love affair for London-based artist Karen Lutchenstein. Her paintings are of objects, treasured possessions and everyday loved items, painted as portraits and filling the canvas. Some of them are in the collection of the designer Sir Paul Smith (see page 206). Rather than buy new, Karen loves to recycle. She purchased part of a temporary 1960s school classroom building and reerected it in her back garden as a painting studio. These impromptu "prefab" school buildings were timber structures with large windows, freezing in winter and boiling in summer, bringing mixed benefits and lasting memories.

BACKGROUND

When Karen needed a new painting studio her preference was to try to reuse items rather than buy new ones. Looking in *Exchange and Mart* magazine, she found an advertisement by a dealer in secondhand sectional buildings. She says, "At the time there was a program of school renovations, and the old sectional 'terrapin' hut [portable] classrooms from the '60s were being bulldozed and [trashed]. The dealer, Victor, sourced several for me to look at over the course of a year, eventually beating the demolition teams to this one at a school in Kent. It was originally 60 x 25 ft (18 x 7.5 m), but we only had room for a 30 ft (9 m) building, so I chose the sections with windows, partly for the light but also for a sense of transparency, which would make it less invasive in the garden."

THE BUILD

The plan was for the dealer and his team to deliver and erect the building, with Karen preparing the site in advance. She built the base of plinths of paving stones and cinder blocks, carefully removing and replanting all the plants to clear the space. And she checked with the council to make sure that the structure would meet legal requirements. "Everything arrived on a lorry, stacked like an old wooden galleon. There were children's drawings still pinned to the walls, flapping in the wind. At first I wondered what I'd done, looking at the heap of mad old wood, but the men knew what to do and it soon took shape. It's made of good, seasoned timber held together with lovely brass screws and collars. We decided not to use the ceiling panels, thus gaining extra height and a sense of space. I later used the panel frames as stretchers for canvas and painted on them. Several are now in Paul Smith's collection."

The roof covering needed replacing with new felt, and to increase the light levels inside, two skylights were added. Some window panes, which had been broken in the move, needed

replacing and the frames required a bit of work, but with regular maintenance they've lasted well. The interior and exterior also needed some remedial work to get them into shape, and it took Karen weeks to pull all the old staples out of the floorboards and to fill the holes before they could be scrubbed and oiled. The outside has cedar cladding, which she painted with black wood preserver.

Services had to be added in order to make this a warm and comfortable working studio. Karen and her partner Will dug a trench to run water pipes from the house, and on the inside they fitted radiators and a boiler. Will's brother helped out by doing the necessary electrical wiring and they insulated the walls and roof panels. When the structural work was finished, Karen and Will, with the help of some friends, planted some trees in front of the building to soften its appearance from the house. From start to finish, the work took about six months.

STYLE NOTES

Karen appreciates the period 1960s architecture and the utilitarian aesthetic of the building – she wanted to keep the essence of that in her studio. She painted it white and sourced the right style of simple, functional furniture, from "here and there," from friends or from her own collection. As she explains, "We love the '60s vibe of the building and it's a pleasing contrast to our Victorian house. Being in the middle of the garden means it feels very calm and private. We see lots of birds and are very aware of the passing seasons."

A folding table tennis table lives inside and when it's not being used for the occasional practice it functions as a large surface for laying out artwork. Most of the furniture is on wheels for ease of movement and to help utilize the space in different ways. Color comes from shelves of objects, art and reference books. For Karen, decorating is a slow process and she prefers to add things gradually as she finds them, her preference being for a room to look as if it's always been there and for the result to feel effortless.

The studio's former use as a prefabricated 1960s school classroom is evident in the design of the building, especially the windows. The space is open to the eaves and two roof lights have been added to increase the light levels inside.

Although many studios are initially created as solitary spaces, it seems that if you create the right sort of space and environment, and then furnish it in a way that is adaptable, it will draw people in, each bringing their own creative expression. The building and its creator are the enabler. Although the primary goal was to build a painting studio for Karen, the whole family also make use of this light, adaptable, creative space. "As well as being my painting studio I run life-drawing classes. All the family members and sometimes friends use the space for filming, photography, music, sewing, film shows and, of course, parties. We built a little kitchen and there's a storeroom with a loft bed."

This garden building has enabled Karen's family to work and play in a way that simply wouldn't have been possible in their house. Karen is keen for the studio to complement the style of their home, and although it's a separate structure with its own atmosphere, more akin to a holiday home, she still sees the house, garden and studio as a visual whole.

151

GLASSMOUNT CABIN STUDIO

For many years the artist Peter McClaren painted in an old coach house that was part of some stable buildings built in a stone quadrangle around a central courtyard. However, although he was not hankering after luxury, the location and aspect of the coach house were not conducive to creating a comfortable working studio and he worried that they might affect his creativity. "In summer, with the doors open, it catches the sun, its light and warmth, but in winter, the sun never rises high enough to provide either. The fireplace radiates very little heat and there's no natural light. I'd never been precious about where I worked, fearful that if I did I might become intimidated by the space."

Eventually, after 25 years of painting in this not ideal studio space he felt that the time was right to overcome these self-imposed restrictions and he had "earned the right" to build himself a proper studio with the right kind of environment in which to work and be creative. "It had to be durable, it had to have light, it had to have purpose and it had to be pretty. If it is not an inspiring place to be in, you are never going to create interesting paintings when you're in it."

THE LOCATION

Peter's family home had plenty of space around it, and in the grounds he identified a possible site with potentially the right aspect to build a new studio. "The site I selected had been largely overlooked. In summer it would be knee deep in stinging nettles, and a winter storm had toppled some trees onto it. For years it had been the spot where we burned our garden and tree waste. However, on the positive side, it had a clear view south between a gap in the mature trees and would catch the sun late into the evening in summer." Work began on leveling the site, sawing up the fallen trees, and carefully removing and replanting the snowdrops and daffodils that were in bloom.

PREVIOUSLY USED MATERIALS

Peter has always been a collector of disused building materials and he had a stash of unusual parts looking for a home, including some pieces of old bus shelter glass that he'd found while taking his car for a roadworthiness test. The yard was earmarked for closure, and the glass would have been thrown away, so the owner was thrilled that he could find a use for it. The glass, having already served time on the local buses, wasn't perfect and, apart from the slime covering it, most of the pieces had graffiti etched into their surfaces, some of which was still readable, including "Pete Loves Eck" and "Rumer Rules. Don't Mess." The size of these glass panes would determine the dimensions of the building itself. The amount of glass and its role in creating a light-filled space was important to Peter: "I wanted to build a space where I could enjoy a plein air experience indoors." The roof on the south-facing side also has two translucent full-length roof panels through which a lot of the interior light is diffused.

He sited vertical posts so that the panes would fit between them and then enlisted his brother's help: up went the structural roof trusses, the floor and walls were insulated, and the interior was lined. In went the woodburner, "turning the space into an oven – it seemed to run on next to nothing and burned the smallest of logs." Inside, Peter built a series of benches around the opposite western end of the building.

"the glass, having served time in local bus shelters, wasn't perfect and, apart from the slime covering it, most of the pieces were etched with graffiti, some of which was still readable . . ."

OUTSIDE

To keep the transgression of mud under control, Peter dug out a path, filling the void with chips from a quarry, and replanted the snowdrops and daffodils in the soil that had been removed in the process. Under the veranda at the front of the studio, logs were stacked to dry, ready for feeding the stove. But he didn't stop there and he even planted a wildflower meadow – the "shed-ow" – with primulas and poppies. "It's a full palette of color, so when you're looking for inspiration, it's outside your door. Watching the crops being planted, ripening and being harvested is all part of that cycle. You also see these great weather systems coming down the Forth."

As the seasons passed the building became less new looking and more established. As Peter explains, "With the arrival of autumn the studio mellowed into its new landscape. The barley crop in the field had been harvested, leaves were falling and the first frost froze the water butts [rain barrels]. The studio has been a revelation and it's been a joy to work in it. With heat and light all year-round, it has changed the way I can work. I could have built it years ago, but I doubt it would have the resonance it has now."

LOOKING BACK

Looking back at this process and where he worked before for so many years, Peter realizes it's the best decision he's ever made. "I had previously been working in the stable yard and had to open the door to get natural light, which is fine in summer, but in winter it was unworkable. It was hard to find motivation to paint with no light and poor heat. This has changed everything – it's perfect. I can even watch the seasons change. The only time I've had trouble with the glare is when the winter sun sets low over the horizon in the west. At the day's end, I'm happy to put down my brushes and just absorb its changing colors."

What he enjoys most about the studio is how it evolved out of its surroundings and how it has mellowed back into them. Peter values the changing light that the seasons bring: "Working within a building that promotes this variety is like adding 100 new colors to your palette."

STYLE NOTES

There is a beautiful symmetry to this building with the repeated identically sized window panes of clear glazed ex-bus shelter glass creating a luminous space that you can see right through, as if only half of the structure is there. It is light, too, within its landscape, and the open veranda continues this theme. Inside, with the open eave space, the lightness continues. The darker varnished floorboards, although practical, also help to ground the space, and apart from the still life reference objects that Peter uses to paint, all the other furniture and objects are white or natural wood or glass. The color is within the art or in nature outside. The simple, angular modern stove complements the repeated squareness of the windows and, together with the chimney and the eaves, creates clean, graphic lines within the studio structure, a useful tool when painting or drawing.

Peter has managed to build an incredibly simple, beautiful and practical studio in which to work. Light is always going to be important to him, and finding and reusing the old bus stop glazing panels wasn't just thrifty and ecologically sound – it was also humorous and witty. The "low art" scratched graffiti marking many a bored schoolchild's long homeward journey on the upstairs of a steamy bus has seen new life in a whole new, more formed artistic endeavor.

ART STUDIO

Rob, a self-confessed "bodger at heart," is a young artist and gardener from Devon. Self-taught as a painter, he works out of a solitary shed studio on a steeply sloping hill on Dartmoor. His paintings are of fictional rural landscapes that "meld with fantasies of an agrarian dystopia," as well as still-life interiors featuring the objects around him.

INSPIRATION

Rob is a true believer in the power of the shed, even declaring that "People with sheds live longer." For him, owning a shed was a necessity: "I needed a place to work that was secluded, quiet and a short walk from home." The inspiration to create the shed/truck came via a friend's gift of Lloyd Kahn's classic book *Home Work*. His first thoughts were to use the shed as a shepherd's hut (in the true sense), but along the way his plans changed and it became a rather less glamorous place.

What he did was to take a classic French military truck and convert it into a "tea/tool nap shed and rusty rubbish storage facility." Initially, his plan was to create a homesteader's plot by buying some land and growing vegetables and rearing pigs. The truck/shed would be used as a real-life shepherd's hut and a shelter for sleeping and tea breaks. And by having one on wheels, he could avoid any potential problems with the local planning department. However, finding a suitable small plot to buy on Dartmoor proved quite difficult, so his plans changed and the truck ended up as a facility for storing scavenged wood and rusty lanterns. "I have a hoard of old windows, nice pieces of wood and bits of rusty iron, and it's also somewhere I can go for a nap. The truck still starts and moves – it was built in 1959 – but the longer it sits still, the more will go wrong!"

Rob likes sheds so much that he has a second land-based shed, sited on the hillside above the truck shed, which is just visible from the bottom of the hill. It functions as his studio space. "The land is owned by my family and they very kindly allow me to keep the sheds there for free."

DESIGN AND BUILD

Rob's approach to design is grounded, contextual and real, and it will resonate with many of us. "I think there's an honest beauty in things that look bodged, wonky and obviously patched and repaired." His first recourse when he needs an object is not to go to the local DIY superstore but to find an alternative item around him that could, in terms of functionality, perform a different task. He explains: "Simple things please me, like a big nail for a hook, a hammer for a door knocker or a bent spoon for a door handle." For Rob, minimalism has no place; he loves to have things around him and appreciates the simple pleasures of a comfortable environment: "Colorful clutter and houseplants make me feel at home."

The construction was a joint effort shared between Rob and his friends. The truck/shed was built from scratch with a few friends in just over a week. The studio shed was built as a shell by a local company, leaving the right-sized holes for him to fit the salvaged doors and windows he'd found in local dumpsters and garbage dumps. He carried each piece, along with the furniture, 437 yd (400 m) up a steep hill.

SKILLS AND MATERIALS

A lover of common sense who has always enjoyed making things, Rob describes his carpentry skills as "pretty basic." A more experienced carpenter friend encouraged him with the established maxim to "measure twice and cut once." Rob still loves a shortcut, and sometimes finds himself using the measurements of forearms, hands and thumbs. He wanted to source as many materials as possible locally to make them relatively sustainable as well as looking good. The timber for building the studio was larch and came from a local sawmill. It is insulated with sheep's wool and has a corrugated steel roof. In terms of the color palette, Rob has a strong urge to paint everything a gloss green, and that was the instinctive and obvious choice for him.

OBJECTS AND FURNITURE

Rob's shed is filled with "strange things that I've found on walks, beaches and in [dumps]. I really like wonky repaired furniture, and the shelves are littered with ceramic dogs, plastic dinosaurs, bird skulls, stones, feathers, rescued plants and old jars. Really, I just like collecting junk. There are also numerous pots of paint and stacks of half-finished canvases."

From his shed he produces his small paintings, which reflect the scale of the studio. "For my paintings I work in acrylics and I have been working mostly on A4 canvases, which are very handy to use when space is an issue. I recently watched a film by Chris Chapman about this interesting old lady who lived in a [trailer] on Exmoor, and he said he was interested to hear that many artists say they would rather work from a shed than a larger room in their house. I don't know why it is, but I just thought that that was obvious and common knowledge."

STYLE NOTES

It isn't easy to find the right space in which to work, and what you ideally want can be costly, while what you can afford may not always be right for you. With a modest budget and a clear view of what he needed, Rob has created a work environment that is affordable, beautiful and in a location that provides abundant source material for his art. His canvases fill the white-painted interior wall panel sizes of his studio and fit neatly onto his workbenches. Paraffin lanterns and other objects for his still-life paintings are clustered on the shelves and hanging from the ceiling. The feeling of both these sheds and the landscape is for Rob one of great natural beauty and freedom.

"simple things please Rob, like a big nail for a hook, a hammer for a door knocker or a bent spoon for a door handle. Minimalism has no place; he loves to have things around him and create a comfortable, colorful home environment . . ."

Rob truly values the "shed" mentality and for him these are truly creative spaces. Inside the buildings he has created an environment in which he can work well, surrounded by bird skulls, plastic dinosaurs, stones, feathers and rescued plants. Even the old paint pot from painting the apple green exterior has been repurposed as a hanging plant pot.

COASTAL ARTIST'S STUDIO

If your day-to-day task is to come up with fresh material and express that through words, art, science or numbers, the crucial constituents of your working environment are the ability to focus, concentrate and stay there long enough to succeed at your task. This artist's studio is a good example. It's set in a beautiful, elemental windswept Atlantic coastal location in Kintyre, Scotland. But just how much of that "outside" is the right amount to allow in? Enough to inspire for sure, together with sufficient good light, which is also a definite. The interior space and how it feels needs to create that level of focus, and how it looks and functions has to be appropriate for the practical processes and scale of the work.

THE PROJECT

The brief for designer Eddie Blake, who was working at the time at Studio Weave (see page 168), was to create a studio that was filled with northern light and set inextricably into the existing geography and coastal landscape. The client's artwork is associated with the location, and they wanted the building to reflect their lifelong connection to the site.

INSPIRATION AND DESIGN

The natural environment here is impossible to ignore: windswept, often wet or snowy, huge skies, notable seasonal changes, rough terrain, huge granite boulders, old stone walls and austere architecture. This is no place for the timid. The fast-flowing stream Allt ant Sionnaich runs through the plot, as does a Victorian "midden wall," which was constructed from dung from the nearby stable block. The three key inspirational elements were the flourishing Scottish Baronial style of architecture, the large granite rocks, boulders and outcrops that punctuate the surrounding landscape, and the characteristic form of the local vernacular agricultural buildings. Studio Weave describes this as "the love child of rock and manor."

With a hard exterior – the twin-gabled structure is clad entirely in cold-pressed zinc panels – the building sits cantilevered over the stream. The sound of the water, whether it's from the ocean, the stream or the rain, permeates it all year-round. The double-pitched structure, in its shape, materials and form, is designed to sit calmly, in a comfortable scale

among the granite boulders. Three large skylights provide the artist's desired northern light while the window openings within the walls focus on specific aspects. And, spectacularly, the internal horizontal surface of the cantilevered section, which is used as a work surface, contains a large trapezoid-shaped glass panel over the stream. This can either be left clear or covered with a section of plywood when a larger work surface is required.

The interior is intentionally minimal; the plan was to keep it clear, clean and simple. Birch plywood covers the walls, floor and roof void, and the goal was to create a simple environment that would enable the artist to immerse himself in his work without distraction. The interior wood panels can also be replaced if needed.

STRUCTURE AND MATERIALS

The structural walls and roof are constructed entirely of timber, with stressed skin panels to avoid the necessity of steel supports. The raw zinc covering was chosen to echo the qualities of the granite rocks, so the walls and roof would weather to resemble them over time. Prefabricated panels were made specially, each as a piece in a precise jigsaw puzzle, which were fitted together carefully on-site. The practical considerations were attached to zinc's durability, gaining a patina over time, and its malleability. And in terms of accommodating any tolerances and to provide space for the façade to be ventilated, the detailed design of the overhanging cornice provided space for these two factors. Each zinc panel was embossed using a cold-press technique in a pattern inspired by Crichton Castle in Midlothian, the more exuberant Palazzo dei Diamanti in Ferrara and Chiesa del Gesù in Naples. As Studio Weave puts it: "It's a dour version of its southern counterparts."

> "the key elements were the Scottish Baronial style, the large granite rocks in the surrounding landscape, and the local vernacular buildings . . ."

STYLE NOTES

With its gray zinc finish and low-gabled roof, the building sits well within its context. However, it has its unique inimitable character, and an unapologetic pride in its uniformity of materials and the paint finish to the door. Internally the continuous plywood covering over the floors, ceilings and walls, work surfaces and bookshelves creates a warm and cohesive finish. The three large roof lights principally light the space, while the smaller "canvas"-proportioned windows in the wall create framed images of nature's own art.

There is a rather wonderful balance here between the artist's internal world and the creation of an inspiring environment and atmospheres that are conducive to the pursuit of their creative endeavors, and on the other hand the stoic, proud and beautiful exterior, which could only seem right in such a precise location. The studio has a striking external armor while accomplishing the task of maintaining a rich interior world. It is very clever indeed.

ECOLOGY OF COLOR

With its unusual patterned exterior, the community-based "Ecology of Color" is a striking building. This large opening and closing timber structure is a community arts studio, birdwatching blind and park shelter all rolled into one. It was designed to explore the role of color in architecture and to express how that, along with form, can create beautiful structures. There is a semioutdoor tiled classroom and storage space at ground level with an enclosed room upstairs offering views of the River Darent and the surrounding trees, while an upper area has shuttered openings. The structure facilitates rustic activities ranging from hidden wildlife watching and foraging to natural dye making, kite design, knitting, drawing and public events that spill out into the park.

THE CREATORS
Studio Weave, an award-winning architectural practice based in London, aims to balance a joyful, open-minded approach to architecture with technical precision. They have a diverse body of work both in the United Kingdom and overseas for public, private and commercial clients.

Most of all, they value idiosyncrasies: "From the characteristics that make somewhere unique to the particular skills of a master craftsperson, we aim to harness the strengths of a project and its team to create something really distinctive and of exceptional quality." Uniquely, they are interested in the relationship between architecture and storytelling, and believe these two strands should be intrinsically intertwined throughout the design process. "In our experience, when these elements work in harmony a rich sense of place can be created. We aim to create immersive magical environments, where the line between practical requirements and imagination is imperceptible. Our ethos is to recognize each project as a transformation, aiming to make a place the best version of itself, playing to its inherent strengths and not imposing preconceived ideals."

THE PROJECT

This extraordinary structure is located in a neglected corner of Dartford and was planned as part of the creation of an "ecology island." The area is a small rural pocket nestling within an urban context at the tip of a wild, wooded peninsula in the heart of this town in northern Kent. The plan was for the creation of a meaningful educational resource, which engaged the community and brought this underused, difficult-to-access and overgrown public area back to life.

The project was guided by the creation of two intertwined cycles: the process of extracting color dyes and using them for crafts, and the wildlife attracted by these plants, including insects and birds. Since its completion in September 2012, the building has become a resource for visitors to explore and learn about plants, insects and birds in all their splendid colors as well as the processes involved in extracting natural color dyes, and the applications of dyes in craft and architecture.

MATERIALS, PALETTE AND PATTERNS

The building uses primarily British woods, with larch for the structural timbers and cedar as the cladding, part of the project's purview being to encourage engagement with biodiversity and celebrate local wildlife. Around the structure a garden has been planted to encourage wildlife and to grow flowers and vegetables that can be used to create natural dyes.

With a terrazzo tiled floor, the sheltered ground floor of the structure is open and accessible to the public as a picnic area or to take cover from the rain, whether or not an event is taking place upstairs. The striking colored square tile-like pattern on the exterior allows the cedar cladding material to show through. The distinctive design is painted with Auro, a water-based, natural wood stain that contains no solvents.

STYLE NOTES

Studio Weave creates structures that use a narrative, making it relevant to the characteristics of the location, the people and the building's purpose. This serves to inform the design process as well as being a means of communication. Here the structure relates to its natural surroundings, and rather than blend in or juxtapose with its clean, graphic colors and the repeating pattern on the walls, it blossoms and is colorful and optimistic.

Even its shape is dynamic, opening and closing as its form changes. It has several stories, including a covered open ground floor and a hinged "beak" on the upper floor where, operated by a simple mechanical pulley system, an entire wall on one side can be opened up, creating the magical effect of being off the ground up in a tree house among the leafy canopy with the river flowing past. This building has an enchanting, adventurous and transformational quality, almost as if it were alive and part of nature itself, having fun out there in the woods.

With its patterned exterior resembling a modern coat of arms, this cedar and larch building has a dynamic open and closing form with changeable features on both floors. The barn-like interior with its opening and closing features has different permutations to engage with the outside or not. Window hatches are either lowered open on chains or opened vertically like French doors, and the upper front wall can fully open to the landscape.

171

FAMILY ARTS & CRAFTS GARDEN STUDIO

Having a special space where every member of the family can follow their creative endeavors (be they art, pottery, sewing or woodworking), and which doubles as a home office and occasional guest bedroom, would check quite a few boxes for most of us. This stylish studio, which has been thoughtfully and intelligently designed and built and is separated from the main house, might look like something featured in a glossy magazine, but actually it's totally practical. Every weekend everyone in this wonderful family comes here and goes into "making" mode, using a wide variety of different skills and creative talents.

THE CREATORS

Amanda Bannister, a UK-based media lawyer with clients in television, fashion and sport, is the mother of three school-age children. Together with her husband, Ed, she lives and works in the city but escapes to their rural retreat in southwest England for weekends and holidays. They love it so much that their long-term plan is eventually to live here all year-round when the children are older. This busy family loves arts and crafts, and they each have their own interests.

AN ARTISTIC SPACE

On the site of a rather tired garden shed Amanda wanted to build a solid, properly constructed building with plenty of light that would take full advantage of the location, with its incredible views over the countryside. The multifunctional structure would provide the perfect space for pursuing the family's artistic pursuits as well as providing guest accommodation. To turn her dream into reality she turned to her friend, the architect George Clarke, who introduced her to designer and craftsman William Hardie.

The simple long, low structure, with a pitched roof, adjoins an outdoor kitchen/pizza oven area and is barn-like in its references. There are two internal sections: the workroom, which contains the pottery, workbench and woodworking areas, and the main living room. Usually both sections are treated as one large open space, but if a more cozy, intimate guest room is required, the large top-hung, sliding, paneled barn door can be used to close off the utility area of the space. In the main section there's a sofa that converts into a double bed, a large table and folding stools. The eye-level windows running along one wall look out over the fields and the natural swimming pond. A wood-burning stove is located centrally on the end wall between two tall, angular windows that mirror the pitch of the roof.

With the woodburner and its angular chimney as the focal points, the main area is a multifunctional space. With the sofa converting to a king-size guest bed it allows for overflow accommodation, and also works as a home office, sitting area with a sofa or crafts space.

The bedside tables also serve two purposes. With the drawers and cupboards front-facing, they contain arts, crafts and sewing materials; on swivel wheels, they turn to reveal a plain back face and visually simpler, more restful nightstand.

INSPIRATION

For inspiration, Amanda looked at an eclectic assortment of buildings, ranging from Scandinavian wooden summerhouses to prefabricated steel Nissen huts, garden potting sheds and even potters' studios. William Hardie's plan was to design a garden studio – a place to work, draw and think creatively. The relationship between the interior and exterior spaces was very important for Amanda, who wanted it to be flooded with light and to relate not only to its context but also to the landscape in which it sits. The interior was to be clean and orderly with all its elements crafted and refined – each item of furniture was designed and built specifically for this building. Amanda knows the environment she's happiest working in: "I like order and calm; light, bright spaces. To work well – professionally or creatively – I need a tidy space." Her goal was to ensure that all the art materials, woodworking tools, pottery equipment, sewing machines and fabric, together with every needle, screw and nail, had its own designated place.

As it turned out, William's and Amanda's tastes were so similar as to be "almost identical," and they both produced mood boards that contained some matching images. It proved to be a highly successful collaborative effort, with Amanda sketching out her ideas on graph paper and sending them to William, who would add his own creative input and then, with his team, work up the details to fully fledged technical drawings. In this way, Amanda's initial proposals were transformed, made to work and brought to life.

"Amanda knows the environment she's happiest working in: she likes order and calm, and light, bright interiors. To work well, be it professionally or creatively, she needs a tidy space . . ."

DESIGN AND PLAN

The design phase covered a five-month period and it cost 10 percent of the entire budget for the project. As Amanda says, "It's so important to spend plenty of time on the design and drawings – a huge amount of planning went into the detail to ensure that everything has a home in terms of storage, that the workspaces were ergonomically designed, and maximum use was made of the view and available light."

The plan was to use a mixture of different woods, retaining some of their grain and color while utilizing specific oils and finishes to create a quieter effect and to tone down any differences between the materials. It was to be an all-wooden, clean-cut building – an example of high-end materials and craftsmanship. Amanda and William were united in their desire to get the best finish, using high-quality woods and real artisanship in the construction of every element of the build from the exterior and interior to every piece of furniture.

MATERIALS AND BUILD

Key to the design aesthetic of creating a calm space with a natural look that fit into its surroundings was the decision to use only wood. Amanda opted for four different types: ash, larch, oak and elm, with different finishes for the shed's exterior, interior and furniture. The plan was to allow the natural charm and beauty of the different woods to take center stage, using prime examples of each one, and by testing different tones, grains and finishes to create an overall harmonious look without losing the original warmth and textures. William and Amanda's approach was more akin to architectural furniture making than the construction of a "shed."

The wide floorboards and most of the furniture are made of oak, the table is elm, and the walls and ceiling paneling are oiled white ash. The sofa has been treated with a floor lacquer with virtually no pigment or shine to produce a finish that, ironically, looks untreated and more akin to its natural state. The cupboard doors are oak, but with the panels set horizontally rather than vertically. Inside, these less precious "working areas" have been constructed from birch plywood in a more utilitarian way. Rough-sawn, textured larch, stained a purply-gray slate color, is used for the construction timber and cladding, while the corner posts and eaves have been left in their natural raw state and will eventually go a delicate silvery gray.

"the plan *was* to allow the natural beauty of the woods to take center stage, using prime examples of each one, and by testing different tones, grains and finishes to create an overall harmonious look without losing the original warmth and textures . . ."

THE INTERIOR

Unusually, the structure of the building and the furniture were approached together. Each element of the interior was carefully considered and was specific to its location and purpose. After sharing ideas and consulting with Amanda, William would draw up the shape, size and design that was right for the space and the item's function before handing it over to one of his craftsmen to add their experience and creativity to the jointing, details and specifics of each piece.

The work was detailed and intricate. Just designing the elm table took 20 different drawings, with William working on the rules and references until he got to the point where he felt the proportions were right and he could designate one of his craftsmen to refine the design. The finished surface is made of tapering-width boards that make the best use of the wood. Fixed with removable timber pegs and wedges, it can be taken apart easily. When you examine it closely, you realize that it has its own "voice" in this unique space and is a true craft solution.

William and Amanda wanted to use boards of differing widths for the flooring and wall paneling, so the oak floorboards are composed of wide planks while the wall paneling is made of narrower planks. This adds visual interest and differentiates between the different woods, making the overall effect less uniform. On each side of the sofa bed, snugly fitting under a cantilevered shelf, is a custom-built trolley on wheels with specific-sized cupboards and three sliding drawers. All the sewing and dressmaking equipment are stored in one cupboard, and the drawing and art materials in the other. In daytime/craft mode the cupboard doors face outwards, whereas in nighttime/guestroom mode they are reversed to create a bedside shelf/cabinet with a simpler finish facing forwards. Everything has been reduced to the bare essentials. There aren't even many decorative objects or clutter other than some books about ceramics, art and design and various pots in different stages of construction.

In spite of all the meticulous planning, this is a simple, uncomplicated space that works on many different levels. Amanda sums it up: "It inspires us to create. It's like entering another world where we can focus on our creative endeavor without the usual domestic, academic and professional interruptions. My son Jack's talent for painting has been rekindled, and my other son Freddy spent a large part of the summer holidays making a skateboard for his best friend. My daughter, Megan, and I have made curtains for her dolls' house, and I've sculpted a piece in ceramic inspired by the potter Hans Coper. Even my husband has been French polishing!"

Amanda's crafts of choice are ceramics and sewing. The shed has been custom-designed to provide her with exactly what she needs for both. This end of the shed is her ceramics area, with specific storage solutions for tools, clay and a kiln as well as work surfaces built at the perfect height for her. Her husband, Ed, has his area of the shed, too, and he loves vintage woodworking tools and likes to restore them to their original condition.

STYLE NOTES

Not only in its style but also in the approach to its design and creation, this building strikes a balance between modernity and tradition. The structure and furniture were considered together right from the start, each with the purpose of playing an equally important part in creating the whole. Studio Hardie likes to "design buildings working from the person outwards," creating unique and specific structures rather than thinking of a form and making everything else fit that model. Each project and its occupants are viewed and treated more holistically as an entirety in themselves.

The care and detail taken in the creation of this unique space are easy to overlook. It looks cohesive, as if all the parts fit together organically and effortlessly. However, the truth is that the amount of thought and planning that were applied here was intricate and phenomenal – not even the tiniest detail was overlooked. Bear in mind that for some surfaces 30 to 40 different wood finishes were tried out before deciding on the correct one. For the white oiled finishes alone, 25 were tested, the aim being to differentiate between the minute differences to keep enough contrast between the different woods while limiting the finished palette. And the oak floorboards were considered a bit too "woody" to stand out against the ash of the walls and ceiling, but by finishing them with a slight purply-gray oil the two wood tones work well together.

At first sight, this highly crafted, light, bright, calm and inspirational space works well and is deceptively simple – but look a little closer. It also gives all the family members the opportunities they need to relax, focus on their work, or work on their individual crafts. It doesn't shout loudly but rather reveals itself and its beautiful considered detail through regular use.

ARCHITECTURAL

Here's a wide-ranging mix of intriguing sheds with different styles, functions, budgets and locations. What they all have in common is a commitment to good design and architectural principles. Many of them have won prestigious awards, like the monolithic twin Eyrie cabins in New Zealand standing off-grid on a remote hillside overlooking the Tasman Sea. In Germany, an innovative "one-man sauna" was nominated for the Mies van der Rohe Award. Its purpose is to change perceptions of urban spaces and culture and symbolize the transition from an industrial to a digitized economy. The Swedish architect Björn Forstberg was inspired by his own mother to design a concept home for the Lingköpingsbo exhibition. It combines intelligent design solutions to make maximum use of a small footprint.

The designer Sir Paul Smith worked with Nathalie de Leval to design a stylish wooden shed that could be flat-packed for easy assembly and transportation. Built from sustainable American ash with a rotating base to enable it to follow the sun, it engages all your senses and encourages contemplation. No architectural section would be complete without a geodesic dome, and artist Alex Hartley has constructed one that can be taken apart and reassembled. This iconic symbol of collaborative living is surprisingly cozy and intimate.

Lizzie Triep and Rowan Moore have created a sinuously curved and cleverly designed "tree house," which is wheelchair-friendly and wheelchair-accessible, behind their home in East London. For architect Niall Maxwell and his partner, Helen, the challenge was relocating from London to the depths of the Welsh countryside and replacing an old barn. Their new build was so successful that it won a RIBA Welsh Architecture award. Sensitive, flexible, practical and timeless, the barn embodies honesty, humility and good design.

And now for something completely different . . . in the frozen wastes of the harsh Canadian winter, an annual architectural competition has prompted a cluster of inventive warming huts for skaters on an icy river. On a lake in central France, an extraordinary floating cabin is a temporary sculpture and art installation. Inspired by Thoreau's remote woodland cabin and the pleasures of living a self-sufficient, simple life, this dynamic space pays homage to his philosophy, referencing his "open-air temple linking earth and sky."

THE TREE HOUSE

The 1830s East London home of the architectural critic Rowan Moore and his wife, Lizzie Triep, was originally two weavers' cottages that were combined to create a single house. In the back garden is a simple, curvy, one-floor, wood-clad addition to the main house. Extending out into the garden, it was built in 2013 as a means of reorientating the family home so Lizzie could remain central to all the activity – whether eating together, entertaining or resting in the garden – as she became more reliant on her wheelchair. She wanted something on one level, which would enable her to "embrace the garden."

THE SPACE

The sinuous new cabin-style extension is visually at home in its back garden location; its low profile, artfully angled roof shape and external vertical cladding establish that clearly. What is clever, too, is the connection between the "tree house" and the main house, whose ground floor is half a story higher than the garden. The architects at the London-based 6a practice explain that the "ramped interior absorbs the half-story difference between the cottages and its new master bedroom and wet room nestled under the eucalyptus tree."

FLOWING FORMS

As accessing the upstairs stories of the house would be time consuming and difficult for Lizzie, the plan was to create a new building that would flow, or drift, away from the original building and allow her to be equally part of the main house activities while providing easy access to her beloved mature garden. Before the build, Lizzie had been unable to do this for two years because getting to the garden meant descending a flight of steep steps. The aim of the build was to make Lizzie feel part of the action. It has a sinuous shape, curving in and out around the Sumac tree with engaging garden views from different vantage points.

ARCHITECTS AND STRUCTURE

Lizzie and Rowan interviewed three different architects before deciding on 6a. Lizzie particularly "liked the way they thought around things," and there was a lot of discussion before they came up with the plans for the tree house. Built on reversible timber foundations with its exterior clad in reclaimed wood, it conveys a sense of the outdoors, of the elements, fresh air and light. Ventilation panels, which, when opened, expose the vertical exterior paneling, allow fresh air to flow through the structure. The large glass sliding door opens longitudinally onto the curvy deck area and into the garden itself. The deck leads into a curving path that Lizzie can easily traverse, and a turning circle allows access in all directions, enabling her

Perpendicular to the main house, the exterior of the tree house is a sinuous, wavy form along the length of the garden. The deck area is equally curvy but in an opposing form. The sloping passageway into the main living space curves along with the shape of the façade of the building. The boundary with the neighbor's fence is angled so as to minimize any loss of light into their garden.

to garden as she moves along it. The construction work, with access provided through a neighbor's garden, took eight months in total. The structure won both the RIBA (Royal Institute of British Architects) London award in 2014, and the RIBA London special award in 2014.

MATERIALS

Built in reclaimed timber, using Australian jarrah and old railway sleepers from a yard in Essex, the exterior of the tree house still bears the holes where the tracks would have been fixed. The building is clad entirely in wood, including the sloping roof area. The interior is lined with pine, simply painted white, and has underfloor heating. The doors, balcony glass and general glazing were custom-made.

THE GARDEN

As the architects note, the presence, the style and the importance of the luxuriously overgrown garden to Lizzie were influential in the design of the tree house. The Sumac tree was shallow rooted with glorious red foliage in the autumn, and when it blew down it was replaced with a new specimen. Heritage plants, including irises and roses, fill the rest of the garden. Looking at the build, your eye travels along the curvy front edge, making the garden feel much bigger. Some of the more established trees needed to be moved, including a weeping mulberry. Lizzie took advice before transplanting it on the other side of the garden, where it settled happily. Other plants included a rose given to her 20 years ago by her mother, and some wild strawberries.

Not wanting to interfere with the light into their neighbor's garden, Rowan and Lizzie made the back of the roof lower, and along the length of the building it slopes downwards, ending at about the height of the dividing garden fence. Over time the foliage has scrambled over the top of this, almost disguising the presence of the tree house itself.

STYLE NOTES

This is no vanity project – it's completely the opposite. It is a very beautiful, clever and yet simple and practical space. Narrow London houses with limited outdoor space do not lend themselves easily to extensions that blend visually either with the house or the garden. However, here the curvy front face, the responding curves of the edge of the deck, and the angled slope of the back of the roof are all gentle on the eye. Materially, too, it's a natural finish, and the foliage creeping over it acts as a form of camouflage so it's literally becoming part of the garden itself.

Access from the house is easy: a pleasant drift down a gently sloping, glazed ramp overlooking the garden. The open ventilation shutters at both ends of the ramp allow the breeze to enter and convey a sense of the outdoors. Painted white throughout, it's a light space in which objects, furniture and books tell the story. The atmosphere is restful while the outlook is calming; you are part of the house and the garden.

For Lizzie it's a special place where she can breathe. She feels that the tree house "has given me back my house." And her favorite spot . . . is in the shade, just outside the doors from the bedroom. A restful, gentle breeze blows there.

The bedroom opens up onto the deck on a continuous level with wide-opening glazed French doors. The deck outside becomes a meandering garden path along which Lizzie can travel and become immersed in and enjoy her garden.

LOW-COST MODERN WELSH BARN

Achieving a life/work balance and finding some space, calm and a great place to live to bring up a young family is the modern conundrum. For architect Niall Maxwell and his artist partner, Helen, part of this conversation was how to move out of London but still maintain the quality of the commissions he worked on. Time spent working for the minimalist architect John Pawson, designing millimeter-perfect, clean-lined spaces for galleries, had set the standard, and quality of work as well as high expectations had to be assimilated into wherever they chose to live.

The idea of relocating to deepest rural Wales came after a conversation with a developer who was buying property there. This stimulus, along with memories of his own childhood holidays, planted the seed for Niall. The journey began towards constructing a self-built modern barn and general multifunctional space, be it home, holiday accommodation, office or studio. Their subsequent project, a newly built temporary home, won the RIBA Welsh Architecture Award Small Project of the Year in 2014.

THE BUILDINGS

There were three structures on the site – a farmhouse, a milking parlor (which has been converted into an office) and an old Dutch barn. The ultimate plan was to convert the old and almost falling-down farmhouse into their family home, but in the meantime the barn, which was in a poor state of repair, was demolished and replaced with a "new barn." This building was to become Niall and Helen's temporary home.

CONCEPT AND DESIGN

The key to the design was dictated by Niall and Helen's desire for simplicity and the necessity of making the barn incredibly functional. They wanted the new building that replaced the Dutch barn to retain its vernacular and be true to its aesthetic legacy, reflecting local and traditional agricultural forms. The design and build were rigorous: precise, neat, simple and uncomplicated. The new barn needed not only to function temporarily as their home but also to be used for a variety of activities when they finally restored and moved into the main farmhouse building.

Describing their new temporary home, Niall modestly says: "It was the two of us bumbling along and things just happened . . . the building that we constructed feels different to the one that would have evolved if we had conceived and built a domestic structure. It's a hybrid between barn, workspace and home – the closest comparison is a loft."

The couple's mindset was "industrial 1980s," to create a simple backdrop for life and for the furniture they possessed. Niall and Helen purchased Scandinavian furniture long before it became fashionable. Their sensibility is artistic, not precious, and the furniture is regularly moved and the space "rechoreographed" and adjusted to create different moods. Their main preoccupation was how to create the essence of the space through the quality of the available light, and to accomplish this they unconsciously referenced Dutch paintings, such as those by Vermeer, where the tonal quality of a space and the light are valuable commodities. This was definitely not going to be a white glaring box.

Niall and Helen wanted to create a flexible family home where the space could be put to different uses. They used simple, humble materials designed with care and architectural principles to retain the essential vernacular feel of the local farm buildings.

THE PEOPLE

Niall and Helen met at art school and their sensibility is, first and foremost, artistic. Tuning into each other and bouncing ideas around is integral to their relationship. Niall had previously been resistant to the idea of leaving the city and investing in a rural community, rooting himself to a place where local traditions couldn't be bypassed. A developer he had worked with in the past had already been converted to this more "folksy" way of life and he feels that he is much closer now to this sensibility. It was a personal but incredibly rewarding journey.

He doesn't want to be "the seagull following the trawler" – he is incredibly driven and passionate and enjoys discovering new things and places, developing in more human terms, reinventing himself by thinking, and exploring and making new stuff happen. Rather modestly, he describes himself as an accidental or incidental architect. However, this wasn't his and Helen's first self-design and build project – they had already built their own house in London, admittedly driven more by economics than anything else.

Almost unstoppable and, without any hesitation, looking for new, sustainable and economically viable solutions, Niall is constantly trying to find new ways of reducing costs. For him, it's incredibly important to be always innovating. "Some of the old buildings we visit have no plasterboard, but there's personality emerging from our investigations." Consequently, this build is all about developing the feeling of a space, not about pristine perfection but harnessing mood and atmosphere.

"it's a hybrid between a barn, workspace and home – the closest comparison is a loft. The mindset was 'industrial 1980s,' to create a simple backdrop for life and for Niall and Helen's existing furniture . . ."

THE SPACE

The new barn was designed to be a flexible space that would allow for changes and adapt to them. Around a central core area that serves as an entrance lobby and two wet rooms are set two main spaces, each with an area of 54 sq ft (5 sq m). Niall and Helen's objective was to create a building that could be used as a whole, initially for their family, or subdivided into two self-catering units. One of the main areas was planned as a sanctuary away from the hurly-burly of family life, whereas the other area was designed with a playroom and bedrooms. However, sometimes the lines get blurred: "The main room is really meant to be a sanctuary for us but, of course, it never works like that – everything gets chaotically mixed."

The large floor-to-ceiling windows provide internal spaces that change as the day progresses. The window to the left of the sideboard is the "morning window" and the dining room table is where the evening light filters through. The family tends to "migrate" to the different areas as the day progresses, with the stove being lit late in the afternoon. And even in the depths of winter the positioning of the southeast-facing window allows a spectacular view down through the valley. The weather here can be inclement, extreme and uncompromising with the prevailing wind blowing from the southwest, and the house often gets a battering. The large "piano" wall was purposely built to tackle this, and the windows are positioned to make the most of the available daylight, radiant warmth and the views of the spectacular landscape outside.

CONSTRUCTION AND MATERIALS

For this self-build project Niall and Helen wanted a means of construction that was easy to erect and clad, without the need for heavy tools and complex engineering. A Parallam frame was templated and machined by a local carpenter, and the timber frame panels were made just down the hill. The materials used brought their own natural palette: stained timber cladding and corrugated sheets form the exterior. The floor is concrete and the internal walls are dry lined while the ceiling is plywood. Heating is provided by two Dutch tile stoves, one in each of the main spaces. The ducting is left exposed in line with creating an industrial, honest aesthetic.

STYLE NOTES

Having a firm aesthetic framework on which to build, create and live becomes an essential manifesto for a successful project. If the idea comes from a good place, is conceptually sound and is born of genuine values, the chance of creating a successful and beautiful space is right in front of you. For Niall and Helen, sustainability, a willingness to work with any budget, no matter how small, and pushing the boundaries creatively in terms of materials are all an important part of their philosophy. The design is sensitive but very real: a nonconformist, honest approach that feels really evident in this unique space. Humble materials are elevated and valued, and the ordinary becomes a little bit extraordinary. The spaces are timeless, and a sense of the Welsh and agricultural vernacular is woven into the space: low light, nothing brash, loud yet sober, peaceful and timeless.

Also importantly, you sense that this couple is happy to take chances – not only because this space was going to be temporary but also because there's an innate freedom in their approach, a confidence in their own aesthetic and what they like. It's all about being resourceful and innovative and not about being a purist in terms of materials. Humble is something they strive for and the atmosphere dictates how the space should evolve. The classical references to Dutch painting are subtly threaded in but restrained; nothing is fussy or overstyled. The design is quietly confident – the spirit of the place and the sense of location are distilled within it. This couple has no fear of changing a space; building in flexibility and good design are a way of life for them.

Its "shed" characteristics reside in its honesty and outward and industrial agricultural aesthetic. This is not a pastiche of a wisteria-clad country cottage but a clean-lined, almost industrial structure, and, in truth, it's just about as integral to farm design as one could imagine. There is no fussy beautification; it's designed to deal with the elements, to make the most of the movement of light and the warmth of the sun, as well as the spectacular views. The interior walls are left unfinished, the plasterboard joints exposed, the wooden structural framework on display, and even the battening is put to work as narrow shelving.

The interior furnishings are beautiful, simple, homely and uncluttered. Against the neutral walls, the rich browns of antique oak furniture are mixed with the lighter tones of midcentury pieces of Scandinavian aesthetic. The decorative items are a mixture of ceramics – charity shop finds and special purchases – intensely colored and independent, while others are clustered together. Framed period landscape paintings are a joyful addition. This may be a new build, but the framed pair of landscapes lightly nod to the past and a more formal agricultural aesthetic. Possessions, shoes, coats and bags are hung up on display – they live lightly and simply without an overabundance of jumble or clutter. This couple relish humility – flamboyance doesn't find a home here. Instead, they are looking for practical, cheap, strong and honest solutions that create beautiful results.

THE WARMING HUTS

During the notoriously harsh Canadian winters, many people in Winnipeg choose to stay inside and go out as little as possible. However, since 2009, an annual architectural competition has provided a unique creative opportunity for the whole community to engage with the great outdoors. The challenge is to design a cluster of small warming huts to sit on the ice of the Assiniboine and Red Rivers, which freeze over in the winter months and are used by the locals as trails for skating. The huts featured here are sited along the Red River Mutual Trail, which starts in a central area known as the Forks where the two rivers intersect, and continues for 4 miles (6.4 km) until it reaches some residential neighborhoods. The effect is to turn the icy river into a frozen park that everybody can enjoy.

THE COMPETITION

Endorsed by the Manitoba Association of Architects, the open competition looks for entries that "push the envelope of design, craft and art." Peter Hargraves, an architect at the local practice Sputnik Architecture, cofounded the contest and foresaw the creative and practical possibilities it created: "This is Winnipeg. We're a winter city . . . let's enhance it." The competition now garners entries from a wide range of practices – from small local ones to the giants of architecture, including, in 2012, even an igloo made from blocks of clear ice that was designed by Frank Gehry himself. The winners are announced every November, and the construction of the winning entries begins on dry land towards the end of January and continues for a week. Upon completion the huts are brought out onto the frozen trail and stay there until the spring thaw sets in, usually around early March.

THE HUTS

The intriguing huts are part sculpture and usually total about 20 and, along with the competition entries, other people are invited to create a hut, and these are sited on the trail along with some selected "greatest hits" of previous years. The huts attract a great many skaters on this busy trail as businesses and local people come together to share the experience of this unique event. There's even a restaurant on the ice to serve dinner to warmly wrapped-up customers who sit on seats made from hide-covered sections of tree trunks under a tarpaulin roof.

Five-hole ice igloo.

FIVE-HOLE ICE IGLOO

Designed by Sam Gehry from the LA architectural practice Gehry Partners, and inspired by the modeling of structures in the office using block-shaped forms, the idea of an open-topped igloo emerged. Double-distilled water was used to create the blocks to increase the structural strength of the ice. As Gehry describes, "The foggier the ice, the more air there is in it and the more likely it is to shear and break if it gets too warm." Some chunks of local Red River ice were included, "which look really great because they have this ephemeral feel to them, sort of blocky and broken pieces." The interior has wooden benches and a central firepit. The structure is crystalline by day and an icy, glowing lantern by night.

NUZZLES

Constructed from hollow, colored foam tubes more usually used in swimming pools, Nuzzles was inspired by the insulating properties of fur. At the core of the structure, in geodesic form, is a mesh of aluminum tubing. The effect is to create an inner layer of still air to keep the resting or "nuzzling" skaters warm.

WOOD PILE

As well as being functional, the Wood Pile serves as an interactive, practical space. The exterior is an open metal mesh lined with chopped wooden logs, which are piled high in preparation for winter. As the season progresses and the logs are burned on the central fire, the walls become lower, allowing passing skaters a better view of the fire and the hut's inhabitants.

THE WIND CATCHER

This playful, angular structure is set perpendicular to the prevailing wind direction, its open tubular section funneling the wind. Inside is a sheltered rest area with framed views of the ice trail. The outer canvas coverings enclose the metal and wooden interior.

Top left: Nuzzles.
Bottom left: Wood Pile.
Far right: The Wind Catcher.

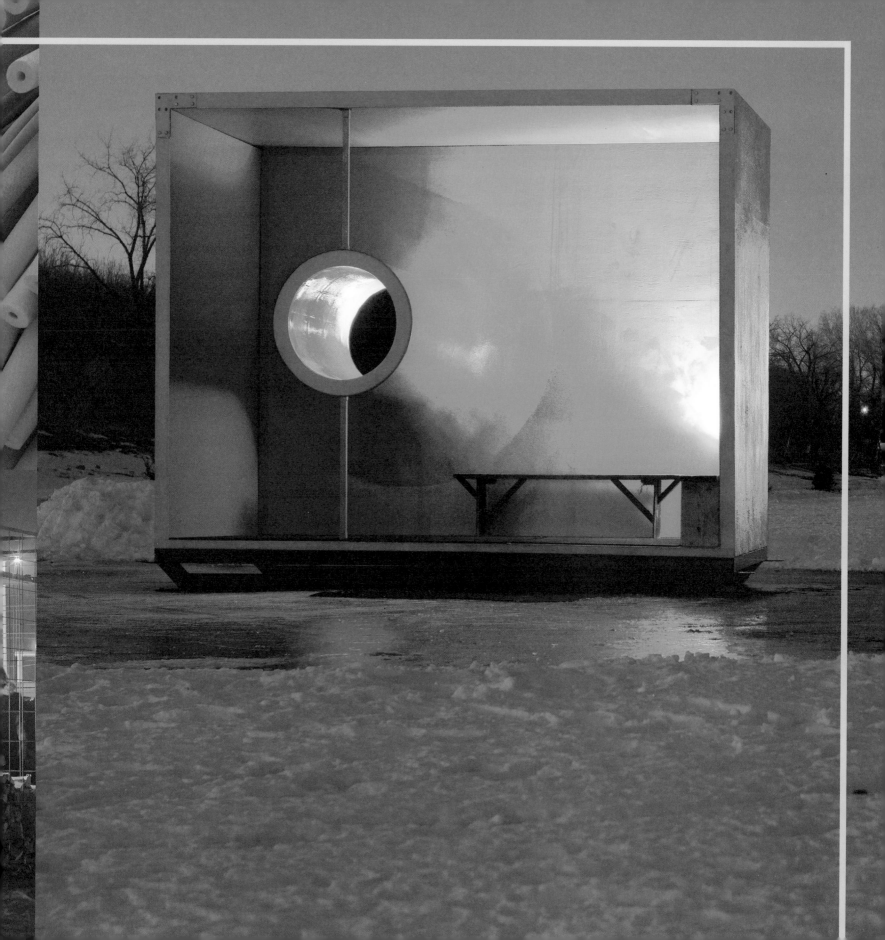

ONE-PERSON SAUNA

The Münster architects' collective modulorbeat created this innovative build as part of a one-year international project and art festival in the German city of Bochum, located in the industrial Ruhr area. It was nominated for the prestigious Mies van der Rohe Award – the European Union's most prestigious architecture prize – in 2015.

THE STRUCTURE
Built on the derelict factory site of the ThyssenKrupp works, the temporary 24 ft (7.5 m) tall tower, which was dismantled at the end of the festival, was constructed from stacked precast concrete parts that were used originally for making shafts. The build consisted of three floors, linked by vertical ladders, with a plunge pool on the first level, a fully functioning one-person sauna booth in the middle and a relaxation room at the top with an open view of the sky.

INSPIRATION
The one-person sauna reflects the philosophy, influences and passions of the architects, urbanists and designers at modulorbeat. Their mission is to work with interdisciplinary projects in urban spaces and to reinterpret their location and change people's perceptions about them by creating temporary, experimental buildings. For the architects, this project symbolized the transformation from our industrial past to the new digital economy of the future and how our attitudes toward urban living, work, art and culture are changing. This structure, designed to encourage both activity and restfulness, was a temporary homage to idleness, inspiring us to consider the future of work in a region where growth has stagnated, unemployment is high and traditional industries are closing down.

THE PLAN
The plan for this symbolic building was conceived in a research laboratory called Borderlands, which examined the peripheral and transit spaces of Bochum as part of the Ruhr urban system. During the process of collating photo collages and texts with a "Do Nothing" theme (referring to the city's response hitherto to its industrial heritage), the architects Jan Kampshoff and Marc Günnewig came up with the idea of a one-person sauna. They wanted to endow the space with a new meaning and sense of purpose, summoning up the energy of the past. The huge abandoned site, covered with grass and young birch trees and crowned by the monumental high tower, would be clearly visible from a distance in different parts of the city, making it an instantly recognizable landmark.

The careful choice of materials references this art installation's heritage of heavy industry in the Ruhr. Precast concrete, black iron and steel are all used within the tower. It has a strong brutalist design aesthetic.

MATERIALS AND BUILD

This was a minimalist structure of concrete, iron, wood and glass, paring down the materials selected to their bare essentials and qualities. The tower was made of slabs of conventional gray prefabricated concrete that resonate with the city's industrial past, but here, stacked haphazardly on top of each other, they were not only functional but objects of beauty, too. The steps and ladders used to reach the interior rooms on the three levels were made of black iron, again reflecting the purpose of the old iron and steel manufacturing factory that had once operated on this site. Inside the tower, the interior walls were bare exposed concrete, their cold austerity contrasting with the warm tones of the wooden sauna.

STYLE NOTES

Although this tower was designed as an artwork, it was also a fully functioning space that really did work – members of the public could book and use the sauna. Inside, it felt small, solitary and enveloping – like a protective cocoon – particularly on the bottom and middle levels where the pool and sauna were situated. You were in control of your environment and had to look after yourself – there was nobody there to help you – but you could meditate and find inner peace and a new sense of your relationship with the external urban environment, especially on the top level reclining on a wooden lounger under the glass roof that opened to the sky.

It was essentially a hybrid and contradictory building: an intriguing mixture of different styles, ages and functions. Industrial and practical in its design and materials, it had a strong aesthetic and was a living artwork installation as well as a fully working sauna; a memorial to the heavy industrial past yet a little oasis of relaxation and reflection in a contemporary urban landscape and high-tech era where new skills and values prevail.

HOUSE FOR MOTHER

This exciting concept home was developed and created by Björn Forstberg, founder of the Malmö architects Förstberg Ling arkitektur & formgivning (FAF), as FAF's contribution to the Linköpingsbo 2017 home exhibition in Sweden. With a floor area of 1,400 sq ft (130 sq m), this unique corrugated aluminum structure is divided into two parallel spaces, consisting of staggered rectangles, with an attached greenhouse. The entry is via a short flight of steps in the junction between the two spaces. Hidden behind the modernist, almost industrial exterior is an airy cabin flooded with natural light. The external shape and silhouette are very traditional, mirroring the archetypal shapes that children make when drawing houses.

INSPIRATION

Björn's mother was the inspiration for this project. She was looking for a new home, and the challenges set by the housing expo gave him the opportunity and motivation to create a special house for her. Japanese architecture and design had always been a great influence on his work, and these are reflected in the simple, clean lines of the finished build.

THE PLAN

This was not a "quick fix" project; the design process started in 2013 with a projected completion date of December 2015. For Björn, "a starting point was to test several ideas I had been thinking about for a while. I'm very interested in raw materials and well-crafted details and, although these are not unique to this project, I hope they give the space some special qualities of its own." To make the most of the available space, intelligent design solutions were sought and used throughout. The larger structure houses the communal living areas – kitchen, open dining and living room – as well as the bathroom and laundry room, while the double-height studio and lofted bedrooms are located inside the second, smaller structure.

MATERIALS AND BUILD

The external walls and roof are covered with raw, corrugated aluminum, which looks austere, slick and cool. In contrast, the supporting timber-beamed construction is left exposed inside and the walls are lined with plywood, making the interior feel warm and cozy. Polished concrete was used for the floor, extending upwards beyond the perimeter to create a bench and shelf. This mixture of simple and basic materials – aluminum, plywood and glulam beams, and concrete – underlines the unpretentious elemental nature of this building. All the materials were chosen for their economical as well as their aesthetic qualities.

STYLE NOTES

The reflective aluminum exterior has an industrial, minimalist quality that belies the warm interior of wood, polished concrete and tiles. The space is light and bright throughout, with understated tones, and the architects made a decision to leave some areas natural while painting others white. This neutral palette enhances the feeling of space even though it is really a relatively small and compact house. There aren't many splashes of color – everything has been reduced to the bare essentials, making this feel like a calm and reassuring place. For Björn, a key concept was to create divisions within the interior spaces by juxtaposing the natural look of the plywood with the white painted areas. The studio is a good example of this: the wall of books is finished in white, contrasting with the natural ply on the surrounding walls, while the ply of the second-story mezzanine level above, housing yet more books, is also painted white.

"Japanese architecture and design had always been a great influence on Björn's work, and these are reflected in the simple, clean lines of the finished structure. Yet, in spite of the minimalist design, the space is spontaneous, warm and inviting . . ."

The plywood finish of the studio extends into the foyer and a small hall leading into the other rectangle, which houses the kitchen, dining and living areas. In the kitchen, unlike the rest of the house, the plywood has been stained a charcoal gray, which contrasts with the dazzling white and warm wooden tones. The white tiled splashback with its distinctive gray grouting mirrors the tiles used on the walls of the bathroom, providing a reassuring continuity. The bathroom and laundry areas are cleverly housed behind the kitchen in their own dedicated space – a gabled-top rectangle in the same shape as the house – literally creating a home within a home.

To create a visual distinction between the dining and living areas and the dividing line between these two functional spaces, Björn simply whitewashed the living room concrete floor and plywood walls. And by morphing the floor on one side into a concrete bench running the length of both rooms, he cleverly blurred the separation and made it more subtle. The white dining table and traditional chairs below the floating white shades of the pendant lighting serve to visually smooth the transition between the two areas.

In spite of its minimalist design, this attractive space contrives to be spontaneous, warm and inviting. It's a manifesto for living a simple yet stylish life. And the juxtaposition of natural wood finishes and clean white floors, walls and surfaces bridges the gulf between the rustic and urban aesthetics, making this an intriguing yet homely build.

Rather than conventional room arrangements, the interior space is divided by using simple architectural forms, different materials and finishes. In the kitchen the plywood has been stained gray whereas in other areas the space has been visually separated either by the plywood and concrete floor being left in a natural finish or by being stained white.

SIR PAUL SMITH'S SHED

For "The Wish List" project, run in association with the American Hardwood Export Council and the London Design Festival, Sir Terence Conran came knocking and asked 10 leading designers: "What have you always wanted for your home but have never been able to find?" Sir Paul Smith asked for a shed. Not just any old shed, but "his shed," and, what's more, he wanted it in its own space – not stuck in the corner of a garden but sitting on top of a hill or on the edge of a forest with an amazing view.

The idea for a shed had come about while talking about the competition to Nathalie de Leval, a furniture designer and maker trained at the Royal College of Art. Along with a shed, they considered some smaller wooden items, such as an easel, but the shed was Nathalie's favorite and very rapidly it became Sir Paul's, too. The decision was announced within a day and the project as a whole was completed in just two months.

INSPIRATION

Sir Paul has always had the ability to find and visualize new ideas and has even written a book on the subject entitled *There Is Inspiration Everywhere, if You Look*. In this case, together with Nathalie, he found inspiration in four places. For him, the main source was the iconic 1948 Mexico City home and studio of the architect Luis Barragan with its large floor-to-ceiling window looking out over his garden. Nathalie, meanwhile, was inspired by some totally different structures: the three-story-tall, black-tarred, fishing equipment drying huts on Hastings Beach in Kent.

Sir Paul's very first shop was in Nottingham and it measured a modest 10 ft (3 m) square. This was the inspiration for the size for the shed – it would mirror the shop where his amazing design journey had begun. Coincidentally, it also happens to be the same size as one of his favorite pieces of art, a Matisse collage known as *The Snail*. And, finally, inspired by the famous rotating writing hut in the garden of the playwright George Bernard Shaw, his shed would have a rotating mechanism that would enable it to turn to follow the sun and the view.

CRAFTSMANSHIP

Sir Paul chose to work with Nathalie because, as he says, "in this highly commercialized world it's so nice to discover someone who is so hands-on, not only in terms of her design but also in the making of her furniture. Nathalie's understanding of the materials she works with is really amazing; she combines this with fantastic craftsmanship to make something truly contemporary." And working with the American Hardwood Export Council and Conran's furniture company, Benchmark, Sir Paul and Nathalie planned to create a shed in sustainable, thermally modified American ash.

With a nod to traditional sheds and barns, this is a beautiful and entirely modern distillation of a simple garden shed. Using thermo-treated ash with a gable end that is completely glassed, the balance is of a perfect solitary space that is connected to the landscape and the outside world.

THE CONSTRUCTION

Both of them wanted the shed to have a natural-textured rough finish. As Nathalie describes it, "Paul and I agreed that the timber should be rough rather than smooth. I visited the timber mill and found this thermo-treated ash. Ash is traditionally fairly white but when treated it goes a deep chocolate brown and is much more consistent. There was just one small pile in the yard and so I decided that was the one." The structure is "in the classic weatherboarding style, so on the outside you get the rough edge while on the inside you're seeing the timber exactly as it arrived in England after it had been thermo-treated, complete with chalk marks and everything, so it's very characterful." She worked with engineer Andrew Lawrence at Arup, an independent consulting firm of designers, planners and technical specialists, to make sure that the shed was structurally sound.

The construction started with the base of the shed. Taking two days to make, it is essentially a shallow wooden box with a solid surface that sits on castors and is incredibly low-tech. Next the framework for the walls was constructed with diagonal wooden brace pieces fitted to create stability. Structurally, diagonal tensioning cables hold the shed in shape and, although simple, they needed to be millimeter-perfect in order for the four-paned large glass wall window to fit exactly. From the framework structure, which is left exposed on the interior of the finished shed, the exterior was clad. The roof interior and exterior were completed in exactly the same way, with no difference in internal or external finishes between the walls and the roof.

MATERIALS, DESIGN AND PALETTE

The Hardwood Council developed a new timber to be used on the outside – pressure- and heat-treated ash, which is resistant to water and mold. Ash is normally whitish gray, but this process turns it dark brown and gives it a lovely aroma, which is similar to roasting coffee beans. As far as Nathalie is aware, this has never been utilized as a construction timber before. Usually it is used only for cladding. Because of the pressure/heat treatment, the wood should have very little or no movement, making it the ideal material for the construction of this shed and enabling them to put detailed design into the smaller elements, such as how the timber was cut and fitted together.

"Sir Paul's very first shop in Nottingham measured a modest 10 ft (3 m) square. This was the inspiration for the size of the shed – it would mirror the shop where his business began . . ."

Both Sir Paul and Nathalie wanted the design of the shed to be like that of a barn. There was very little wastage of wood during the build because of the way the timber was cut. It wasn't sanded or planed and the cladding was shiplap. In the detailing, nothing was made smooth – they wanted texture. It is honest to the language of a traditional shed – it's not insulated and has been traditionally built apart from the glass wall and rotating base.

A traditional shed always begins from the base, adds the walls and, finally, places the roof on top, but this innovative build had to start from getting the glass wall right, then the rotating base, and the rest of the shed followed. They had to engineer this design because of the need to flat-pack it (in a sophisticated and highly skilled way) and move it easily from location to location (specifically for exhibitions and the Victoria & Albert Museum in London). Nathalie makes models of all her designs, usually out of a softer material than the final design, and this helped her to get a feel for the finished space.

THE CHALLENGES

The biggest challenges for this project were how to create the full wall of glass and the structural works. The design was essentially simple, and it was important to stay true to that and not to overcomplicate or overengineer the structure, so the finished shed would look effortless. The project was sustainability measured and checked, too. Everything used to build the shed had to be weighed and this information was utilized in a life-cycle analysis; that is, what was used to build it compared to how long it is expected to last.

ATMOSPHERE

The atmosphere Sir Paul wanted to create was one of contemplation. In the beginning he thought the space could become his workshop, but now he wants it to be a place to which he can escape. "It's not the type of shed to be shoved into the back of a garden by a compost heap. It needs a view and the sun to follow." The wood smelling like roasting coffee beans, the tactile materials that look and feel natural, and the design all combine to engage your senses, enhancing the atmosphere of the project. The color of the material is uniform and honest, and the interior space feels larger than you imagine. And, of course, when you are standing inside the shed, the glass wall draws your attention and you immediately focus on the view.

WALDEN RAFT

This see-through floating cabin was designed by Elise Morin and Florent Albinet as a temporary sculpture and art installation for the 2015 Horizons Arts-Nature festival. Floating serenely on Lac de Gayme in France's Auvergne region, it can be moved manually via a rotating wheel and cable running from the shoreline to an anchor in the center of the lake – the same principle as used by cable ferries with a windlass mechanism.

INSPIRATION

Elise and Florent were inspired by a remote woodland cabin built beside Walden Pond, Massachusetts, by the nineteenth-century American writer Henry David Thoreau. He lived there for two years, two months and two days while he was writing *Walden; or, Life in the Woods*, his revered account of self-sufficiency and the pleasures of living the simple life. They both admired Thoreau's philosophy, and the concept behind this design was to create a really dynamic space that would pay tribute to his ideas and encourage reflection and contemplation.

THE PLAN

The cabin is built on almost the same latitude and to the same proportions as Thoreau's original hut: 13 ft (4 m) high and 107 sq ft (10 sq m). The plan was to design a structure that would bridge the gap between Thoreau's "walled-in space" and the great outdoors, creating interaction between the internal and external environments and integrating seamlessly into the landscape. By adding buoyancy, mobility and transparency to this mix, the cabin could shift and be transformed with the movement of the water, the weather and the seasons. What this couple wanted to create, in essence, was a "nonspace," which would readjust to changing conditions and would neither be private nor public property – in Elise's words: "not entirely outside the world, nor entirely interiorized; it is an intermediate space, a lookout post where one can see while accepting to be seen."

MATERIALS AND BUILD

The walls and pitched roof were constructed from sections of traditional pine and contemporary transparent acrylic glass panels, mounted on polyethylene floats and connected with rope screws. Both primitive and modern materials and techniques were used and allowed to mingle. At 2,645 lb (1,200 kg), this raft is not only robust but also surprisingly heavy. Its transparency is deceptive and it looks a lot lighter than it is. Recyclable acrylic panels were chosen rather than glass as they are lighter, more transparent and consume less energy. As Elise says: "The combination of wood and a modern industrial material, acrylic glass, brings transparency to the build while maintaining its protective function."

This unique structure has been designed to foster reflection and contemplation. Open to the air, it has a solid base while the upper section has only a partial material construction. It is minimal but interesting, open yet enclosed, a complete structure but it's not all there – an intriguing dichotomy.

STYLE NOTES

The cabin is completely empty apart from the rotating central wheel that moves the raft away from terrestrial life on the shore to its buoyant aquatic environment. Inside this extraordinarily tranquil space, the light is diffused by the transparent acrylic panels, and if you half close your eyes the haphazardly scattered panels of wood almost appear to be levitating. It is childlike in its simplicity, an escape from the bustling real world, and a place where you can rediscover your inner self and take time out to just chill, relax and dream. For Elise, it's "a model of the primitive habitat at the birth of architecture . . . the beginning point of any house." However, you don't inhabit this cabin – it is part of a very special and specific relationship with the land and the water. Above all, it's a space for experimentation – a "floating, luminous, audible and mobile vessel."

The cabin is illuminated at night like a shining mirage hovering over the dark lake against the dense blackness of the surrounding forest. Integrating and melding into the landscape, the Walden Raft is defined by its trajectory, which underlines the horizon, and by its reflection in the lake, referencing Thoreau's "open-air temple linking earth and sky." This modern makeover of his basic cabin in the woods is an enchanting floating "shed" where it's great to spend some contemplative quality time and just daydream.

211

WALDEN RAFT

GEODESIC DOME

Alex Hartley is a respected British artist who works on large-scale outdoor artworks and has long had an interest in community-based living and utopian ideology. He takes his work into the public realm, expanding the context. Aesthetically and practically talented, Alex has always made structures and dens, alongside his sculptural work.

THE PROJECT

Alex's plan was to build over a six-month period, using scrap metal car panels, a demountable geodesic dome that could be transported in sections on a truck between locations. It was exhibited at his 2011 exhibition at the Victoria Miro Gallery. He was inspired by Drop City, an early artists' and architects' hippy commune in Colorado, where they built and lived in structures based on Buckminster Fuller's ideas and theories. He wanted to use the cheapest sheet metal available, so car hoods and roofs were the material source for constructing the triangular sections of the dome. American cars tend to be bigger than UK models, with larger panels for cutting and creating the segments for making a geodesic dome. As he says: "About three triangles can be cut from one car top. UK cars only yielded one triangle and modern paint finishes made finding suitable metal quite a task." The completed dome would be moved and reerected in different contexts and locations.

BUCKMINSTER FULLER AND GEODESIC DOMES

Described as "one of the great minds of our times," R. Buckminster Fuller worked across several disciplines: architecture, design, geometry, engineering, science, cartography and education. Describing himself as a "comprehensive, anticipatory design scientist," he believed in looking across disciplines to find pioneering solutions to universal problems, in "doing more with less," and making the world work for all humanity.

The geodesic dome, which was first shown to the public at the 1954 Milan Triennale, was one of his major themes and is believed to be among the most efficient forms of human shelter. The dome-shaped building was made up of triangular segments whose shape gave them "unparalleled strength." The internal volume comprised the largest amount of interior space contained by the smallest possible surface area. Along with this material efficiency, the spherical shape allows air – both warm and cool – to circulate efficiently throughout.

DROP CITY

The original 1960s Drop City in Colorado was a commune of counterculture artists. This potent symbol of the hippy movement began with great energy, a sense of purpose, good principles and earnest geodesic dome building by its artist community members. The commune had no rules and the dome building drew a lot of public attention, winning in 1967 the Buckminster Fuller Dymaxion award for their geodesic constructions. However, after some time, internal tensions surfaced between the founding members and the second wave of residents and the commune disbanded. Nevertheless, it has remained an iconic symbol of collaborative and creative artistic living, social experiment and utopian pursuit.

THE CONCEPT

Alex was inspired by Drop City and he planned to move his dome, assembling and disassembling it, to different locations, not as an expression or a performance but more as a *tableau vivant*, a mix between a still image and a stage play. He wanted it to appear as though he had reinhabited an abandoned dome from the hippy era. His idea was to have chickens and other accoutrements of self-sufficiency, spending the exhibition days living in the structure. It was important to him that it felt authentic, like an original dome from Drop City. "I imagined that the commune had broken down and been abandoned and I had discovered it and moved in. The materials and styling all took their lead from this premise." Even the color palette would echo his inspiration and evoke the original abandoned domes. He wanted it to look rusty and faded, and true to the originals the exterior has continued to fade and weather with the passing of the years.

There are existing and available plans for geodesic domes, and it's possible to create them in different sizes. This build needed to be big enough for a small family but not so large that it couldn't be moved or remain intimate in scale. The size of each triangle also had to be proportional to the scale of the scrap car roof panels.

BUILDING AND DISMANTLING THE DOME

The building and dismantling process requires six people to manhandle each of the eight large sections, designed to tessellate and fit into a truck. They have to come apart, so they have breaks to allow disassembly. To assemble the dome the pieces are set around the circle shape, propped up and tipped slightly back. Alex describes the next stage: "The tricky bit is to tip them in so they sit together with the metal triangles overlapping on the outside. Some hammering is needed to bring everything together and then the inner structure can be bolted." When the "side" walls are complete, the top sections are pushed up the outside of the dome and propped up from the inside.

After several moves, the dome started to leak due to the intense hammering that was required to get everything into shape. Because of the way the rain runs down, it's difficult to trace where the leaks are, but this problem has now been ironed out. An assembled dome is a strong structure that can withstand high winds. In fact, geodesic domes were the only buildings to survive unscathed from the epicenter of Hurricane Katrina in 2005.

LOCATIONS

Alex lent the dome to the antiglobalization Occupy movement in the City of London to be used as a meeting place, but before long the pattern of Drop City repeated itself. The dome was waterproof and more comfortable than the rest of the temporary camp and drug users took over the space. Its second installation was rather more peaceful, as part of an exhibition of Alex's artwork at the Victoria Miro Gallery in London. He built a platform at the rear of the gallery over the existing canal and the dome was reerected on top of this, with Alex living inside on-site for the duration of the exhibition.

With its surface created from triangular sections of metal cut from old car roof panels, Alex built this movable structure as part practical space, part social experiment and part art installation. The usual approach to furnishing doesn't apply because there are no entirely straight walls inside, forcing you to think afresh and to use more of the floor space or adopt new solutions, such as the hammock shown here.

215

EYRIE CABINS

These dark little cabins won the 2014 Home of the Year award for the New Zealand–based Cheshire Architects. For Nat Cheshire, the designer, this place changed everything. "It took all the things I believed in and compressed them into a hard core of concentrated form and space. I really love it here and that's very unusual for me. When the cabins won the award, it gave them a reason for being that extended beyond ourselves."

SUBVERSIVE STRUCTURES

The wooden, monolithic twin cabins stand off-grid on an inlet of Kaipara Harbour overlooking the Tasman Sea north of Auckland. Anonymous and surprisingly small – each with a footprint of only 312 sq ft (29 sq m) – and with their exteriors burnt black, they look more like boulders scattered randomly on the green hillside than houses. They are exciting, innovative and subversive – they don't have any doors and you have to climb over rocks to get to them, entering through a window. As Nat puts it: "We hoped that in subverting the shorthand language of building, these little constructions might feel like something other than – and more than – houses."

AN ALTERNATIVE VISION

Nat was inspired by a different and alternative vision for New Zealand's coastal heritage. For him, architecture is a total practice and he is invigorated by the potential of all its forms. In his own words: "I am committed to aggressively exploring the breadth and depth of architecture, and to inventing its future." This project is a case in point. His young clients wanted a retreat from the intensity of their urban lives: "Some place small and humble and yet very powerful – powerful enough to break the memory of the city."

A MODEST BUDGET

There were severe budgetary constraints on this project and Nat's solution was to design two very special but small houses that, unlike many larger buildings, would each have its own very forceful singularity. "Something that felt more like an object than a building, tethered and quietly bobbing on its sea of grass." Together with the owners, he sought to draw a rich quality of experience from the modest budget. They were unflinching in their commitment to quality, even if it meant abandoning scale and amenities to achieve it. Nat says: "We all pushed each other to the limit of what was achievable, manipulating the budget and project down to the tens of dollars in pursuit of that perfect tipping point – just before humility falls into poverty."

The challenge of the scaled-down floor plan was overcome by focusing on the essentials of everyday life. Each structure has two large openings: one serves as an entrance, the other as a window, framing the view of the estuary beyond. There are wooden hatches for ventilation

and a skylight for gazing at the starlit canopy – there is no light pollution in this isolated spot.

The cabins are oriented towards the best panoramic views of the distant coast on one side and the verdant hills on the other. The original plan was to site them on top of the hill, but Nat decided to build them closer to the water, which would not only help protect them from the wind but would also make them feel "an intimate part of this beautiful landscape rather than something watching over it."

MATERIALS AND BUILD

Distinctive charred cedar boards were used for the exterior of the cabins. Nat was inspired by the work of the abstract painter Kazimir Malevich, and he wanted to blacken and stabilize them rather than saturate them with chemicals and oils. What the charring has delivered is an incredibly soft-rough finish, which feels organic and emanating from the land rather than synthetic and imposed. The black theme is repeated inside one of the cabins with the interior linings and cabinetry constructed from black form-ply. The idea was that in a tall black space you could lose the boundaries between different surfaces, such as the walls and ceiling. It's akin to sitting inside a drop of ink or in deep space. Even though it was a small project in construction terms, the build took a long time. The local builder fit it in around other work, which demanded enormous patience on behalf of the client, but the end result made it all worthwhile.

STYLE NOTES

This really is off-grid living. There's no designated road or paved pathway and you have to walk through the rustling long grass, carrying your weekend bags and provisions, to reach the cabins. When you arrive and climb up the pull-down steps to enter through the window, there's an amazing sense of the infinite housed within a very small space – the high ceilings help create a feeling of spaciousness and prevent you feeling claustrophobic. Above the living area is a bedroom loft, making maximum use of the available space. Even though the black surfaces in one of the structures seem to merge and blend into one another, a variety of refined textures is still distinguishable. The form-ply has a lovely gleaming and slightly tarnished finish – even though it's a throwaway product, it's well crafted and effortlessly takes center stage.

The kitchen space is light and airy, excavated from the exterior black mass of the cabin. The unlacquered brass kitchen bench and surround shine out like jewels among the more simple wooden materials. The walls are a rough, light-colored plywood with no adornment whatsoever. The high ceiling is also constructed from the same ply and matches the color of the floorboards, making you feel as though you are inside a wooden box but connecting with the natural world outside via the enormous opening in the wall. At first glance, this is a simple scheme with precise pieces of furniture and finishes, and a natural palette, but look more closely. Stylish and elegant, it's a version of minimalism in which, instead of decoration, clean-lined sculptural shapes and careful material choices are used. The interior might be modest but it pays attention to the outside world with large square window openings that are reminiscent of artworks.

This is a remote place and these quiet, contemplative spaces are a fitting response to the isolation of this beautiful environment. There is something very restful about these diminutive black boxes. They are the perfect retreat from city living – somewhere to chill out, reconnect with the natural world and discover what's really important in life. And they prove that even with a modest budget you can still create really extraordinary spaces.

HOMES

More and more people are building or converting their cabins and sheds into affordable homes. Applying the principle of "less is more," they are often motivated by a desire for a simpler and more honest life in a smaller space or for hand building their own custom-made dwelling. If you have a small budget and plenty of time on your hands, this can be the ideal solution to acquiring your own home. In the process, you can even create your own narrative and add your character and personality to the build.

This was the case with Axel, who hand built his own inexpensive A-frame house and "Humpy" on a plot of land in Tasmania. His gradual step-by-step approach to building, together with his revulsion of banks and loans, meant that it took him several years to finish the job, but the end results are charming and engagingly rustic. For Axel, the ongoing process was evolutionary, and an advantage of constructing a home in this way meant that he could be flexible, think out solutions to problems as he went along, and rebuild, improve, adapt and make new additions as the need arose.

On the other side of the world in the heart of rural England, Rupert and Jude Hunt set about renovating an old stable on their farm. To preserve the essential character of the building, they used their clarity of vision and a "gentle touch" to breathe new life into it, replacing only the essential parts that had fallen down or crumbled with age – in this way, they retained its aesthetic imperfections and intrinsic rustic feel. For this enterprising and creative couple, the budget is less important than how the house is put together and "how it feels."

And lastly we feature an extraordinary build in Ireland that was specially designed and constructed for two installation artists. This tilted, mirrored house with its angled roof and reflective walls intrigues the viewer with its capacity to appear and then seemingly to disappear into the surrounding, ever-changing skyscape and landscape. One moment it's there and then it's gone – the reflective surfaces create a spectacular visual effect. It's a clever and very effective concept as well as a functioning and stylish family home.

THE MIRROR HOUSE

This intriguing tilted, mirrored house, with its angled roof and walls designed to reflect more grass than sky, is the home and studio for two conceptual artists. Almost camouflaged in its rural landscape, it was designed by the Irish architect Dominic Stevens for Grace Weir and Joe Walker. Having become acquainted through mutual friends and parties, they visited the house that Dominic had built for himself in the same region. The commission for this build came from there. As both Grace and Joe work on installations and video, it made sense in the first instance that the house was designed with respect to the ideas in their work.

INSPIRATION

Dominic believes that architecture is more to do with people than buildings: "We just make beautiful places for them to do all the stuff that they like to do." He also subscribes to the view that good architectural design is essential to society and that architecture should not be perceived as a luxury item, affordable only by the rich. While on vacation in Paris, he was inspired by a retrospective of the American conceptual artist Dan Graham, whose mirrored pavilions embody visual and cognitive reflection and transparency. Grace's work was an influence, too. At the Venice Biennale in 2001 she showed a piece of work, a cloud filmed from either side of a helicopter, and projected both views onto opposite sides of a gallery wall.

THE "INVISIBLE HOUSE"

Spectacularly "there" but "not there," the external form of this 1291 sq ft (120 sq m) house and its reflective surface create a unique visual effect. The reflections give the fleeting impression that the house appears and then disappears into the sky and the landscape. The glass is, in fact, both reflective and transparent. The house doesn't alter the landscape in which it sits; rather, the constantly changing landscape and skyscape transform the house. Its structure is angular with a sloping roof and you approach it across a field and enter through a cutting. In this unique entrance ravine, the hillside becomes the front door.

EARTHWORKS

By entering the house on the lower level, down the ravine, it feels as though you are going underground. The downstairs bathroom and master and guest bedrooms are on this level. Both Grace and Joe work from different spaces at various times, and small computer workstations are tucked into corners in the earthworks below.

From here you continue your journey into the house via a spiral staircase to the contrasting lighter upper living and eating floor, where through the façade there's a filtered view of the surrounding hills and countryside. The interior is white and, with the angled roof shape, the ceiling heights are varied, ranging from 6 to 14 ft (1.8 to 4.2 m), prompting you to question your sense of scale and judgment of three dimensions. The large, flexible space upstairs is good for spreading things out, for the stuff of general living, and parties.

As the sun moves around the building during the day, the room changes as you orient yourself towards the light. The large landscape vistas are viewed as a captured image, reminiscent of a back-projected photograph. The glass used to create this effect has been considered as a material in its own right rather than just something that fills a window – it is semireflective and designed for solar control. From the outside the building looks like a reflective angular solid, and you can look through into the interior, more so as the external light fades.

AN ACCIDENTAL HOME

The initial plan was to create an economically built rural retreat, away from the couple's Dublin flat and studios. As Grace explains, "It just kind of happened. We accidentally moved to the country." The limited budget was extremely small and the goal was to create something "ambitious and counterculture." When the house was finished Grace and Joe moved in and never moved out. They had a daughter, too, by then, so changing the house from a minimal chic space into more of a family home made sense. And although it hadn't been designed as such, the house adapted well to the change in the style of use. "It's become our absolute fascination – watching the way the landscape and sky are continuously changing."

STYLE NOTES

Incredible for its use of materials as well as its inspiration and application of conceptual art, this building is a part of the landscape and the human experience of it. The site retains its agricultural function, producing food and fuel as it has done for hundreds of years. The lower floor, almost part of the ground, is vertically timbered, simple and strong looking. The semireflective mirrored upper floor and tilted exterior walls are effective, whichever side of the internal/external viewpoint you are looking at it through. It is simply made more so by the tilted angle at which it is set.

It isn't a complicated structure, nor is it decorative or nostalgic, and it certainly isn't conventionally rustic or rural, but it is unique and extraordinary. The landscape is reflected, the house disappears and the landscape is magnified. It calls attention to itself and then does just the opposite – it's a very clever building indeed.

THE HUMPY

Axel's passions lie with people and nature. After working in environmental management for several years, he's now studying to be a social worker. His interests range from politics and social justice to building, gardening and microhouses. He puts into practice what he preaches and applies his principles and interests to the realities of his life and home.

As he says: "I think it's important not to expect everything to happen overnight and to be perfect – I'm happy to live with the mistakes I've made when building. And I don't rush into things and want immediate gratification and results. Wanting something *now* is expensive. It takes the fun out of the creative process and is a disease of modern times."

THE CABIN

When he bought a plot of land in Tasmania with a ramshackle structure on it, Axel called it the "Humpy," an Aboriginal word for a nonpermanent dwelling. It was constructed out of different building styles and materials. He worked on it over several years, tackling the insulation, timberwork, windows, doors, deck and heating. During this time he worked his way through the tasks, learning new skills as he went along. "I learned to build there. I'm mainly self-taught, and living off-grid without a generator in the early days I was limited to just some hand tools, a chainsaw and a cordless drill. I added the windows by simply sticking the chainsaw through the wall and working out how to put a window in."

For Axel, building is an ongoing evolutionary process, stage by stage as his funds allow. The challenges are the limiting factors of building regulations and the sheer hard work that's involved in elemental building – eventually you just run out of energy. However, he was helped in his endeavors by his community of friends, and outside of the work they had a lot of fun, sharing "big feasts, beer and wine."

THE THINKING PROCESS

Using the analogy of building as a step-by-step progressive process, Axel compares it to "Lego for grown-ups. Thinking of building a house is challenging, but by breaking down the building process into little steps, they all suddenly seem very achievable. I always find it best to visualize what I would like to change: staring at a wall and picturing what it would look like if I went through it to create an extension, or if I added an additional window, or built a permanent structure next to the shower, say, where I could plant a jungle of herbs."

CHALLENGES

Alex says that his skills have developed over the years. "Generally I've learned from my mistakes and from my friends. The main challenges are living on a building site while I'm working there and continuing to work regular hours at the same time. Starting building work when I come home from work after 5 p.m. and then working until midnight becomes exhausting after a while. Weekends are often spent just doing building work with little or no relaxation, during the building and renovation periods."

Most of the building materials that Axel uses are timber. He especially likes reusing "specialty" woods when he can get his hands on them. He has toyed with cordwood masonry and rockwork as well.

THE CREATIVE BUILDING PROCESS

For Axel, building is a creative process in itself, and the work has its own tempo, with all of it happening stretched out over spans of years. Stage one is quick – a period of intense work over a three- to four-month period while the house/dwelling is built – but over the subsequent years new ideas occur and the changes and revisions begin. So meanwhile he saves up and starts again. This is a cyclical process, which "seems to happen every four years."

When his energy levels drop, he loses creativity. "When I start building I almost always have ideas that do not eventuate in the end. Sometimes I come back to them later on after I've had a break from building. I stick to about four months of building at a time. This makes it easier not to lose energy. The greatest challenge is to keep that energy and not lose the passion."

STYLE NOTES

The palette throughout this unusual structure is predominantly white, which makes a small space seem bigger. It also offsets the use of a lot of timber, which can become claustrophobic. Splashes of green add some finishing touches to complement the surrounding eucalyptus trees. Collected objects from Axel's extensive travels are scattered around the space as well as family pieces of sentimental value.

"I'm happy to live with the mistakes I've made when building. And I don't rush into things and want immediate gratification and results. Wanting something 'now' is expensive and it takes all the fun out of the creative process . . ."

The Humpy has been described by some visitors as custom-made and eclectic. Looking at this hand-built, hand-crafted countryside cabin you can see it as an ideal in Instagram – the perfect light, a romantic glow and the ideal escape from the material world. However, it can also be viewed as a spartan-like existence or simply as an honest and affordable family home. Whichever you prefer, it demands your attention and is remarkable insofar as it was built by one man and his friends and molded over time as and when he got inspired and had saved the necessary funds to carry on building.

It's an honest structure, not only in its affordability but also in its use of materials and resources. Rough clad and hand sawn, it isn't insulated from the everyday minutiae of real life. Like the exterior, the interior is hand built and contains all the basic necessities. Warmed by an old wood-burning stove and decorated with textiles and books, it has a simple appeal that isn't hard to recognize.

A-FRAME HOUSE

A-frame houses are simple and relatively inexpensive to build. Popular in the postwar period, their sides are steeply angled, meeting at the roofline. Resourceful Tasmanian resident Axel is not a novice to building and has his own inimitable style. Not wishing to engage with bank loans and debt, he favors a step-by-step approach, when he can afford it. Rustic and hand built, this is the second house he has built on this site.

He had been living in the Humpy (see page 226) but the local authority required him to put up a new building, according to council regulations. Alex was reluctant to do so because he didn't have the funds to build another home afresh, so he needed to think and work creatively. "I stalled the council's request to build for more than a year while some architecture students I knew drew up the plans for me."

A TRUTHFUL JOURNEY

Stage one, the initial structure for the A-frame, was built within nine weeks. The immediate priorities were to have a nonleaky roof, an efficient space to heat and the necessary council-approved sign-off. However, this solution wasn't perfect: "The house was initially fairly dark and it turned out that the design would benefit from being mirrored. The pantry, bathroom, storeroom and WC were on the sunny side while the living area was on the shady side."

Over time Axel made the necessary changes. This wasn't a place that he loved initially and it took time and many changes before its appeal really grew on him. "After four years I swapped things around, making the house a lot lighter. And after four more years, I made a slight extension for a staircase and moved the compost toilet inside. For me, building is always an ongoing evolution. I don't like banks and loans. As a result I built according to my saved budget – save again, and build again. It was an ongoing process involving new ideas and more tinkering."

It took Axel eight years before he fell in love with this house. "Initially, I built mainly with secondhand windows and the design wasn't great. An A-frame without roof windows can be a bit dark, and the rooms on the west side should have been on the eastern one. After two additional rebuilding, improving and adding-on projects, I grew to love this place."

CHALLENGES

During the main build period, Axel's friends would turn up every day to help him. "There were people who had never held a hammer in their hand before, while there were others with a car full of tools. There are parts of the house where that is quite obvious, but I'm happy with that. There were some days when I had as many as 15 people helping out and every evening after sundown we ate together and drank a lot of home-brewed beer."

Even with this level of help, however, there were always the challenges of living every day on a building site, surrounded by plaster dust, sawdust and piles of building materials and all the inevitable mess.

Building in winter was particularly challenging. At one stage the roof was off on one side of the house for three nights and Alex could see the stars above him. "My mate, who was living in the Humpy at the time, could talk to me from his deck while I was lying in bed. Frost settled around me for two out of the three nights. It was a freezing winter, and with open noninsulated walls for some time while we were building, most mornings the thermometer read just 36°F (2°C)."

The A-frame house has a large ground-floor living space but smaller rooms as you climb up to higher floors. Over time, the space has been modified to extend it outwards and to add a staircase and windows. The build and finishes are in timber from the local sawmill, each part weathering in its own time.

THE CHANGES

To get the building from lockup to the final approval stage by the local authorities took another three weeks, but it was still a work in progress. In order to make the space more appealing and comfortable four years later, Axel changed half of the rooms from the west to the east side of the wall with the objective of making the interior a lot lighter. He also built a basement because the house is raised on stilts and he needed a guest room as well as storage for his garden produce. And another four years later he extended the building yet again to house a staircase, which enabled him to build walls upstairs and to make even better use of the available space. The composting toilet also went into the extension and he replaced all the windows. At last he can say: "I love it now and think I might be done."

MATERIALS

Using mainly timber and plaster, the 60-degree A-frame house gradually took shape. For the interior, when he could get his hands on them, Axel liked to reuse "specialty" timbers, and a great source were the scrap timber woodpiles at his local sawmills. He says he has "used timber that was milled on my block and even though it's beautiful, the thickness varies remarkably, making accurate work difficult. I have recently started using pallets which I use whole or pull apart. I always keep an eye out for secondhand building materials, such as doors and door furniture. I replaced all my secondhand windows with new double-glazed ones. The old ones were simply too cold, but they are perfect for extending the greenhouse, so they aren't wasted and everything gets recycled again." And with the wood, too, Axel used a specific approach to the interior carpentry: "Inside I tried to avoid right angles wherever I could, including the cupboards and benches, which are not square."

"I don't like banks and loans. As a result I built according to my saved budget – save again, and then build again . . ."

STYLE NOTES

In Axel's words, "This is no town house." There are reddish-brown timber and warm colors throughout – red in the kitchen and yellow in the dining room – while most of the walls are painted white and the color is provided by the rugs and textiles. The A-frame structure means that the large ground floor creates a spacious living area, with the narrowing upper story used as bedroom space. And in terms of design, here it comes with a meaning. Axel thinks it's cozy: "Someone said that every level, every room holds a surprise. There are lots of knickknacks and collected memories here. Overall it's very busy."

The furniture, too, is homebuilt, and there are textiles, materials, pictures, photos and flyers from years of traveling to festivals and cultural events. Character and personality are valued, and it doesn't all have to be tasteful – it's the story and the meaning that are important. Even the "tacky German bits and pieces" have earned their place, and the flyers from festivals collected over many years are the wallpaper in the toilet.

THE OLD STABLE

With the idea of working hard and putting in the hours while they are still young and then using the capital and experience earned to create a more rural-based life/work arrangement, Rupert and Jude Hunt bought a tumbledown wreck of a beauty of an Elizabethan farm and outbuildings aiming to create a home, a place to work and an income as a "cool country escape." The 400-year-old agricultural and Grade II listed historical Old Stable is one of the outbuildings, and this enterprising couple devised a plan to restore and convert it into a twenty-first-century part venue and hangout room. They wanted to create an atmospheric space that was authentic, inviting and nostalgic with a real sense of the past – a place for contemplation, sharing and talking the night away where people could enjoy each other's company, drink, sing and just relax.

THE CREATORS

Rupert and Jude met at university and worked in London and then Asia before settling in Bristol and bringing up a young family. They decided that the time had come for them to "cash in the chips" on all that drive and endeavor, and after investigating rural enterprise possibilities with yurts and tree houses they settled on bricks and mortar and bought a rambling Tudor farm in rural Shropshire – a place that was so in need of work that no one else would touch it. However, inspired by their travels and their skill set – Rupert had run his own interior design company and Jude managed a design agency – they took on the challenge.

For them, the buildings had everything they needed: the main building had enough room for a good-sized conversion as well as subsequent earning potential. And it was Elizabethan timber-framed "chocolate box cute." The outbuildings, including the Old Stable, were untouched and large enough to potentially bring in a good revenue stream. It was the first of the properties they viewed. Jude stayed outside feeding their baby in the car while Rupert investigated, and as soon as he stepped inside the house he proclaimed, "I have found my bar," and that was it.

THE RENOVATION

All three buildings on the site were renovated: the farmhouse, the barn and the Old Stable. They were all Grade II listed historical buildings and none of them were habitable. Rupert and Jude tackled the main house first, then the barn and, finally, the Old Stable, which formerly had housed donkeys and ponies. Initially, their plans were to completely renovate the building, including adding glazed panels to the front and installing a new kitchen and bathroom, but over time they were captured by the nature of this beautiful ancient structure. Rather than create a new radical interior and jeopardize its essential character, they opted for a gentler touch, which would keep the building "alive and safe" for as long as possible, to enjoy its unique character and real beauty. As Jude says, "Our belief in this as our objective grew the longer we lived here and better understood the place and its past."

It was not an easy task. The building was so old that it was almost unrestorable, and as soon as the couple started to take something away, something else would fall down. And as soon as they replaced one thing, they'd have to replace something else as well. In the end they decided to stay as close to the original feel as possible and breathe new life into it by replacing only the absolute worst part – the front that had weathered so badly. Their solution was simple wooden paneling that echoed the original and would weather down well to complement the

"Rupert was covered in grayish brown dust and dirt for a week. It took a lot of baths to wash it off. It was a very emotional time and to be able to restore the first building he had fallen in love with was a wonderful thing . . ."

rest of the exterior. They particularly loved the wrought-iron side panels and didn't want to touch these. Their plan was revised and adapted to one of maintaining the structure and its stability while finding ways to make it as similar to how it used to be as possible, while enabling its use as a space for entertaining.

While they were trying to maintain its ancient beauty, the building had seen 400 years of hard use and muck, and the structure needed underpinning and a new concrete floor poured in. A wood-burning stove was added for warmth and atmosphere. Rupert did most of the work himself, along with Tony, the lead builder who had worked on the other buildings, and he was covered from head to toe in grayish brown dust and dirt for about a week. It took a lot of baths to wash it away. It was a very emotional time and the work took about a month, but to be able to restore the first building he had fallen in love with was a wonderful experience.

Where and whenever possible, the materials existing on-site were reused in the restoration work, much in the same way that things would have been done over the centuries. For instance, old horseshoes that they found on the farm were used to strengthen the joints between the timbers while tin from the main house's old roof was recycled to repair the stable roof, and the tiled section was repaired using rejected handmade tiles from the farmhouse. Nothing was wasted and everything found its place.

THE OLD STABLE

INTERIOR

Staying true to the intrinsic natural and rustic feel of the barn and its genuine color palette and traditional textures, Rupert and Jude purchased most of the furniture at flea markets or local auctions with the exception of the long elm table, which was handmade by Tony the builder, his plan being to create "a Bavarian beer table with a natural twist." The chairs are old ones salvaged from the local pub, and many of the other items were found at farm sales – even the sheepskins came from local sheep.

Acquired over time, with references to their travels, especially in Asia, Rupert and Jude's style is flexible enough to encompass new experiences, tastes and colors, absorbing them along the way and developing their own taste. As Jude says, "I think that spending so much time in atmospheric locations, absorbing all the color and the Asian sensitivity to the palette provided by nature, must have rubbed off on us hugely. All I know now is that as soon as I walk into a room I either feel it or I don't. And that's never to do with money. Or culture. Or city or country. It's to do with how it was put together and how it feels."

STYLE NOTES

The ability to create "atmospheres" and spaces that engender a specific feeling, mood and purpose is a skill that comes partly from the person creating it and partly through the architecture itself. Rupert and Jude had always enjoyed hosting fun, social occasions and creating a good ambience, so they decided that they wanted to earn a living from their home doing exactly this.

In practical terms the Old Stable had to keep its beautiful imperfections. Its restoration came as the last piece in the jigsaw of renovating all three rural buildings, and although the couple were exhausted, they had learned a lot, worked hard and lived in a trailer with their young family for two years. Although this could be perceived as a drawback, in actuality it enabled a clarity of vision to keep the raw, original, rough and rustic beauty of the stable there to be enjoyed. It also engendered a belief that in creating an atmosphere, the items selected need not be expensive. Instead, by following your own nose and taste, any object, painting or piece of furniture to which you are drawn is worth a second look.

239